Good News

Long Division

and

Multiplication

John Mark Liggett

Copyright © 2015 by John Mark Liggett

No part of this publication maybe reproduced, stored in a retrieval system, or transmitted in any form or by any means, except as permitted by United States copyright law, without the prior written permission of the publisher.

ISBN 978-0-9968572-0-8

Published by John Mark Liggett
Jose Agular Street, Barili, Cebu 6036, Philippines

About the author: John Mark Liggett received a Bachelor of Science degree with a major in mathematics from the University of Illinois and became a Member of the American Academy of Actuaries (MAAA). He has designed and implemented data processing systems for insurance companies and done computer programming in the following languages: assembler, C, and C++. The Good News multiplication and division algorithms were created in 2010 for his nine-year-old son.

Table of Contents

Section	Page
1 Why This Book Was Written	1
2 How to Use This Book	6
3 Basic Arithmetic Operations	10
4 Doubling	16
5 Table of Multiples	19
6 Numbers in Expanded Form	22
7 Short Division	27
8 Good News Multiplication	30
9 Multiplication Examples	35
10 Good News Long Division	46
11 Division Examples	70
12 Fast Track	82
13 Methods Compared	84
14 Blank Grid Forms	87

Section 12 contains a two-page summary of the Good News multiplication and division algorithms, which may be enough to learn them.

1 Why This Book Was Written

Elementary school children often have considerable difficulty learning traditional long division because it requires skills that these children have not yet developed. Traditional long division requires that each quotient digit be estimated and then tested with multiplication. Third and fourth-grade children may be more than two years away from the age at which their prefrontal cortex has developed sufficiently to do the type of thinking that estimation requires.

According to Jean Paiget's theory of cognitive development, most third and fourth graders are in the "concrete operational stage," roughly ages 7 to 11. The mental abilities needed to make good numerical estimates probably do not develop until the "formal operation stage," which usually occurs after age 11 and continues into early adulthood. The Good News Long Division algorithm fits fourth graders' concrete operational stage perfectly while the estimation required by traditional log division requires mental abilities that do not develop until they are older.

By the fourth grade, most children know how to add, subtract, and compare numbers pretty well. They are also practicing the multiplication tables and beginning to do long division. However, ***traditional long division requires children to use the process that they learning to "estimate" each part of the result of that same process.*** They must repeatedly ask themselves "how many times does the divisor go into," or divide, some other number in order to find each quotient digit, which then must be multiplied by the divisor. Making good estimates about a complex process requires a thorough understanding of it, considerable practice in using it, and formal operational thinking. Those learning long division lack all of these prerequisites. Consequently, the long division process quickly degenerates into a tedious and frustrating guessing game that involves plenty of error-prone multiplication to check the guesses. Furthermore, the process is so frustrating and laborious that it does little to improve estimation skills.

Why This Book Was Written

An example of a traditional long division calculation that might be encountered late in the fourth grade is shown at the end of this section. Please note the column of multiplication carries above the divisor. These numbers are not always written as shown in the example. Instead, the student may mentally calculate each one and try to remember it while multiplying the next two digits to which it must be added. The next few paragraphs describe what might happen when a fourth-grader tries to determine only the first quotient digit shown in the example at the end of this section.

The problem is to divide 190480 by 248. In order to find the first quotient digit, several steps are involved. Starting with the left-most (high-order) dividend digit and moving right one digit at a time, dividend digits are linked until a number is formed that equals or exceeds the divisor. In this case, 1, 19, and 190 are less than 248, but 1904 exceeds 248. The next step is to find out how many times 248 goes into 1904. In other words, the student must now somehow either divide 1904 by 248 or estimate the result of this division – and this is where trouble starts.

One common method for estimating quotient digits involves rounding both the dividend and its divisor to their nearest high-order digits and then dividing the rounded dividend by the rounded divisor. In this example, 1904 is rounded to 2000 while 248 is rounded to 200. Next, 2000 is divided by 200, and the result is 10. However, this result cannot be correct because it has two digits. And so, very early in the division process, estimation fails to be much help. There are probably other estimation methods that might be attempted, but these methods are beyond both the scope of this book and the grasp of most fourth-graders.

Nevertheless, we will keep at it, just as fourth-graders are expected to do. Since 10 is too big, the next logical estimate for the first quotient digit is 9; but 9 times 248 equals 2232, which is also too big. The student now tests 8 as the first quotient digit, but the product of 248 and 8 is 1984, which is still too big. Finally, the digit 7 is tested and found to be the correct first quotient digit because the product of 7 and 248 is 1736, which is less than 1904 while the product of 8 and 248 is greater than 1904.

Why This Book Was Written

However, the correct first quotient digit of 7 will not be found if an error has been made when 248 is multiplied by either 8 or 9 and the product is found to be a number less than 1904. Such an error can easily happen in several ways including: (1) incorrectly mentally multiplying two digits, (2) picking the wrong multiplication carry from others noted above the divisor or recalling the wrong carry from the prior multiplication, (3) incorrectly adding a carry digit to a product, (4) making a transcription error when writing the product of the quotient digit and the divisor beneath 1904, and (5) incorrectly subtracting this product from 1904.

Unfortunately, errors like the ones described above are usually not discovered until the long, complicated division process is completed and checked by a multiplication process that is almost as long and complicated. The student finally learns that something went wrong only after the dividend fails to equal the remainder plus the product of the quotient and the divisor. However, the student still does not know whether an error or several errors have occurred in the division, in the multiplication used to check the division, or in both of these calculations. The only way to find out what went wrong is to repeat both of these lengthy, error-prone calculations without making any more mistakes. In fact, these calculations need to be repeated at least twice because the general rule for checking results is that same answer must be gotten twice in a row. Obviously, the traditional method of long division is a big problem for most elementary school students.

Some educators have chosen to solve this problem by no longer teaching either long division or multiplication by more than one digit because the algorithms are "just too difficult." Instead, their students are taught to use electronic calculators. The problem with this solution is that it provides a poor foundation for those who want careers in science, technology, engineering, and mathematics (STEM). Learning to use a calculator for multiplication and division does not develop the sound understanding of these basic arithmetic operations that is needed for a good foundation in mathematics, which is the "language of science." Furthermore, children get the message that they really cannot do very much without a calculator. The message that they should get is that mathematics is about understanding logical relationships, and not about pushing a certain sequence of keys on the current model of an electronic calculator.

Why This Book Was Written

Fortunately, **some good news** can be found in this book. The **only skills needed** to learn Good News Long Division and Good News Multiplication are the three skills that third-graders already have: **adding**, **subtracting**, and **comparing numbers**. Furthermore, **no multiplication** is involved in either process, which entirely eliminates a major source of errors. The long division process is greatly simplified because it requires **no estimation** or trial-and-error guesses of successive quotient digits. The long division process can be **easily checked** as it is performed so that errors are found and corrected long before the final result is reached. Students also learn about the fundamental nature of both multiplication and division.

The primary motivation for this book is the difficulty children have with long division. The Good News Long Division algorithm, which is the emphasis of this book, was developed first. The Good News Multiplication algorithm followed later. *Good News Long Division and Multiplication* was written to provide elementary school students everywhere with a simpler, easier alternative to the traditional methods of long division and multiplication. Children are much more interested in subjects when drudgery is eliminated and confusion is replaced by clarity.

Why This Book Was Written

Traditional Long Division Example

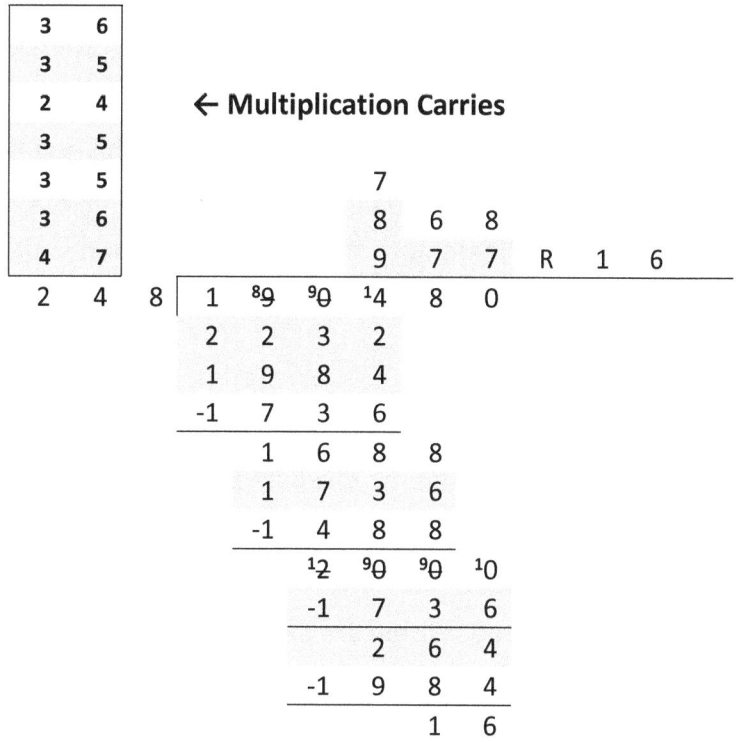

The shaded areas are the results of incorrect quotient digit guesses.

2 How to Use This Book

This book can help someone with high-school-level math skills teach third and fourth-grade students how to do whole number multiplication and long division. It is not a self-study manual for elementary school students. The teacher or tutor needs to learn these algorithms before teaching them to others. The best time/age for students to learn Good News Multiplication and Good News Long Division is soon after they have mastered the single-digit multiplication tables because at this point students usually have adequate understandings of addition, subtraction, comparing numbers, and the place-value number system. (Please note that **no multiplication** is used in either Good News Multiplication or Good News Long Division. Also, **no estimation** is needed for Good News Long Division.)

Whole number arithmetic does not involves either decimals or fractions. In whole number arithmetic, the result of dividing 16 by 5 is a quotient of 3 with a remainder of 1, and not 3.2 or $3\ ^{1}/_{5}$. However, the algorithms presented in this book are easily extended to decimal numbers and mixed numbers in the same way that traditional multiplication and long division are extended to such numbers.

This book has 14 short sections. Much of the material is optional. The reader should look it all over and use whatever is helpful. Section 12 is a two-page summary of both Good News Multiplication and Good News Long Division. Both of these algorithms can be learned by studying only section 12, so it might be a good idea to look at this section first. However, information throughout the other sections of this book are important. It provides additional explanation and insight into the theory and suggest ways of avoiding calculation errors. A brief summary of each section of this book follows on the next page.

How to Use This Book

Section 1 tells why this book was written.

Section 2 tells how to use this book to learn the Good News algorithms.

Section 3 reviews the names of operands and results for addition, subtraction, multiplication, and division and covers some basic arithmetic concepts.

Section 4 describes a simple addition technique for doubling numbers.

Section 5 tells how to use doubling to produce the "table of multiples," which is necessary for both Good News Multiplication and Good News Long Division.

Section 6 explains how to write numbers in a special expanded form, which is needed only for Good News Multiplication.

Section 7 describes "short division," an efficient division method for single-digit divisors.

Section 8 describes Good News Multiplication and gives a step-by-step example of how to do it.

Section 9 gives Good News Multiplication examples of increasing difficulty.

Section 10 describes Good News Long Division and gives step-by-step examples of how to do it.

Section 11 gives Good News Long Division examples of increasing difficulty.

Section 12 summarizes the essential ideas of both Good News Multiplication and Good News Long Division with a one-page description and example of each.

Section 12 tells how to check the results of Good News Long Division.

Section 13 compares Good News Multiplication and Good News Long Division to the traditional methods of multiplication and long division.

Section 14 provides blank grid forms that can be copied for practice problems.

How to Use This Book

The following steps are suggested for learning Good News Multiplication and Good News Long Division:

1. Practice the following skills in order: doubling numbers, building tables of multiples, and expressing numbers in special expanded form. Start with single-digit base numbers and add digits until 5-digit base numbers can be handled quickly and accurately. Check results with a calculator. See sections 4, 5, and 6 for examples of these procedures.
2. For Good News Multiplication, reproduce the examples in section 9. Create additional practice problems if necessary, and use a calculator to check results.
3. For Good News Long Division, reproduce the examples in section 11. Create additional practice problems if necessary. Practice problems can be created as follows:
    a. Choose a divisor, quotient, and remainder at random, or with specially chosen digit patterns;
    b. Use a calculator to multiply the quotient by the divisor and then add the remainder to get the dividend for a practice problem.

Example: Choose divisor = 215, quotient = 3,210,011, and remainder = 1;

Dividend = 215 x 3,210,011 + 1 = 690,152,365 + 1 = 690,152,366;

Problem: 690,152,366 ÷ 215. Answer: 3,210,011 R 1.

The computational difficulty of traditional multiplication and long division increases dramatically as the number of digits in the multiplier or divisor increases. By contrast, the difficulty of the Good News algorithms increases only slightly as these operands get bigger. Consequently, students move quickly and easily from problems that have small operands to those with much larger ones.

Grid paper should be used as students begin practicing the Good News algorithms so that the main focus is on learning the procedures and not on keeping columns of digits properly aligned. Section 14 contains blank grid forms that can be copied for practice problems.

How to Use This Book

Mastery of the Good News algorithms occurs when problems with 4-digit multipliers or divisors can be calculated quickly and accurately. After mastering these algorithms, a few problems should be done every month or two for about two years so that the algorithms are firmly embedded in the student's long-term memory. After the fifth or sixth grade, students should probably be using calculators most of the time for multiplication and division so that they can better focus more difficult concepts.

Please note that mathematics tends to be a very visual subject, so don't let the words used to describe a procedure get in the way of understanding it. "A picture is worth a thousand words," but the thousand words that create a clear picture for one person may utterly confuse another. The best approach may be to do the following: (1) study an example and try to understand it, (2) read the description of what is happening in the example, and (3) return to the example and try to reproduce each part of it with a pencil, paper, and calculator.

The "good news" of this book is that students can now be spared the drudgery of long practice sessions using the complex, error-prone methods of traditional multiplication and long division and still gain a good understanding of how these arithmetic operations really work.

The inequality symbols shown in the table below will be used in this book.

Inequality Symbols			
<	Less than	>	More than
≤	Less than <u>or</u> Equal to	≥	More than <u>or</u> Equal to

3 Basic Arithmetic Operations

The arithmetic operations of addition, subtraction, multiplication, and division each act on two numbers called operands to produce a result. These arithmetic operations are shown below. The names of the operands are shown in the shaded areas while the names of the results are shown in bold letters. These names will be used in later sections of this book.

	Addition			
	3	4	5	Addend
+	2	6	7	Addend
	6	1	2	**Sum**

	Subtraction			
	7	0	2	Minuend
−	4	1	3	Subtrahend
	2	8	9	**Difference**

Multiplication

		3	4	5	Multiplicand
	x	2	6	7	Multiplier
9	2	1	1	5	**Product**

Division

Quotient ↓   ↓ Remainder

                      3   8   R   3

Divisor→   2 9 | 1   1   0   5

                  ↑ Dividend

Note: The result of whole number division is both a **Quotient** and a **Remainder**.

Additional Comments for Subtraction

Good News Long Division requires subtraction because division is simply repeated subtraction. The traditional method of denoting borrow activity is shown below.

$$\begin{array}{rrrrr} ^6\cancel{7} & ^9\cancel{0} & ^9\cancel{0} & ^{17}\cancel{8} & ^13 \\ -2 & 9 & 7 & 8 & 6 \\ \hline 4 & 0 & 2 & 9 & 7 \end{array}$$

Abbreviating borrow activity helps eliminate extraneous marks that clutter the calculation area. The borrow activity above can be abbreviated as shown below.

$$\begin{array}{rrrrr} \cancel{7} & \cancel{0} & \cancel{0} & ^1\cancel{8} & ^13 \\ -2 & 9 & 7 & 8 & 6 \\ \hline 4 & 0 & 2 & 9 & 7 \end{array}$$

The figure above should be interpreted as follows.

$$\begin{array}{rrrrr} \cancel{7} & \cancel{0} & \cancel{0} & ^1\cancel{8} & ^13 \\ \downarrow & \downarrow & \downarrow & \downarrow & \downarrow \\ 6 & 9 & 9 & 17 & 13 \\ -2 & -9 & -7 & -8 & -6 \\ \hline 4 & 0 & 2 & 9 & 7 \end{array}$$

For digits 1 – 9, a crossed-out digit means one less than the digit that is crossed out while a crossed-out zero ($\cancel{0}$) means 9.

See →	$\cancel{1}$	$\cancel{2}$	$\cancel{3}$	$\cancel{4}$	$\cancel{5}$	$\cancel{6}$	$\cancel{7}$	$\cancel{8}$	$\cancel{9}$	$\cancel{0}$
Think →	0	1	2	3	4	5	6	7	8	9

See →	$^1\cancel{1}$	$^1\cancel{2}$	$^1\cancel{3}$	$^1\cancel{4}$	$^1\cancel{5}$	$^1\cancel{6}$	$^1\cancel{7}$	$^1\cancel{8}$	$^1\cancel{9}$
Think →	10	11	12	13	14	15	16	17	18

Please use this borrow notation if it is helpful. However, it will not be used later in this book so that unnecessary distractions are minimized.

Additional Comments for Multiplication

The **multiplicand** is number of things in a group, the **multiplier** is the number of these groups, and the **product** is the total number of things in all the groups.

Multiplicand	x	Multiplier	=	Product
(Group Size)		(Group Count)		(Total)
12		6		72

If a there are 12 chairs in each of 6 rows, then there are 12 x 6 = 72 chairs altogether. The group size is 12, the group count is 6, and the total is 72.

The multiplier tells how many multiplicands must be added together to make the product:

$$12 \times 6 = 12 + 12 + 12 + 12 + 12 + 12 = 72$$

Additional Comments for Division

The dividend is the total number of things to be put into groups of equal size, the divisor is the size of each of these groups, and the quotient is the number of divisor-sized groups that are contained in the dividend. The remainder is the number of things left over after removing as many divisor-sized groups from the dividend as possible. The remainder is always less than the divisor.

The quotient can also be viewed as the number of times that the divisor must be subtracted from the dividend to get a final difference that is less than the divisor. The example below shows how to use subtraction to divide 14 by 3. The dividend is 14 and the divisor is 3. The quotient is **4** because the divisor must be subtracted from the dividend or its remaining value four times to get a final difference that is less than the divisor. The remainder is the final difference of **2**. The remainder must always be less than the divisor.

$$14 \div 3$$

					↓	Subtraction Count
14	–	3	=	11	1	
11	–	3	=	8	2	
8	–	3	=	5	3	
5	–	3	=	2	4	← Quotient
				↑		
				Remainder		

Additional Comments about Multiplication Carry Activity

Multiplication carry activity is a major source of error in both traditional multiplication and traditional long division calculations.

Traditional Multiplication

```
              6  3  1
              3  2  1        ← Multiplication Carries
              2  1
              3  7  4  2
           x  9  5  4
        1  1  1                ← Addition Carries
           1  4  9  6  8
        1  8  7  1  0  0
     3  3  6  7  8  0  0
     3  5  6  9  8  6  8
```

Traditional Long Division

```
  1  2  3
  1  3  4                         ← Multiplication Carries
  1  4  5
     1  2           3  7  6  4  R  3
     2  5  8 | ⁸9  ¹⁶7  ¹1  1  5
             -7    7   4   0  0  0
                   1   9  ⁶7 ¹1  1  5
                  -1   8   0  6  0  0
                       1   6 ⁴5 ¹1  5
                      -1   5  4  8  0
                           1  0  3  5
                          -1  0  3  2
                                    3
```

Note: Traditional subtraction borrow notation is shown below the division symbol that separates the divisor, dividend, and quotient.

Additional Comments for Traditional Long Division

The figure on the following page shows the series of subtraction operations that produce a quotient and remainder, which are found as follows.

Given a dividend and a divisor, repeat the steps below until the remaining dividend is less than the divisor. The initial remaining dividend is the given dividend.

1. Find smallest series of high-order digits in remaining dividend such that number formed from these digits is greater than or equal to divisor.
2. Find **by some unspecified means** largest single digit such that product of this digit and divisor does not exceed step-1 number. This digit is quotient digit. Its place value is same as last dividend digit used to make step-1 number.
3. Subtract product of divisor and step-2 quotient digit from step-1 number.
4. Make next remaining dividend by appending step-3 difference in front of dividend digits to right of last dividend digit used to make step-1 number.

The quotient equals the sum of the products of the step-2 quotient digits and their place values. The remainder is the final step-4 difference.

The major problem with traditional long division is finding the step-2 digit, which involves trying to determine how many times the divisor goes into the step-1 number. In the example on the next page, the trick is to find out how many times 258 goes into 971, 1971, 1651, and 1035 to get the quotient digits 3, 7, 6, and 4. Finding these quotient digits often degenerates into a very frustrating trial-and-error guessing game with plenty of error-prone multiplication to check the guesses while trying to find the right step-3 product.

Good News Long Division uses a very simple device to eliminate all the problems inherent in step 2 above. This innovation eliminates all estimating/guessing of quotient digits and all multiplication from the division process. (See section 12.)

Additional Comments for Traditional Long Division

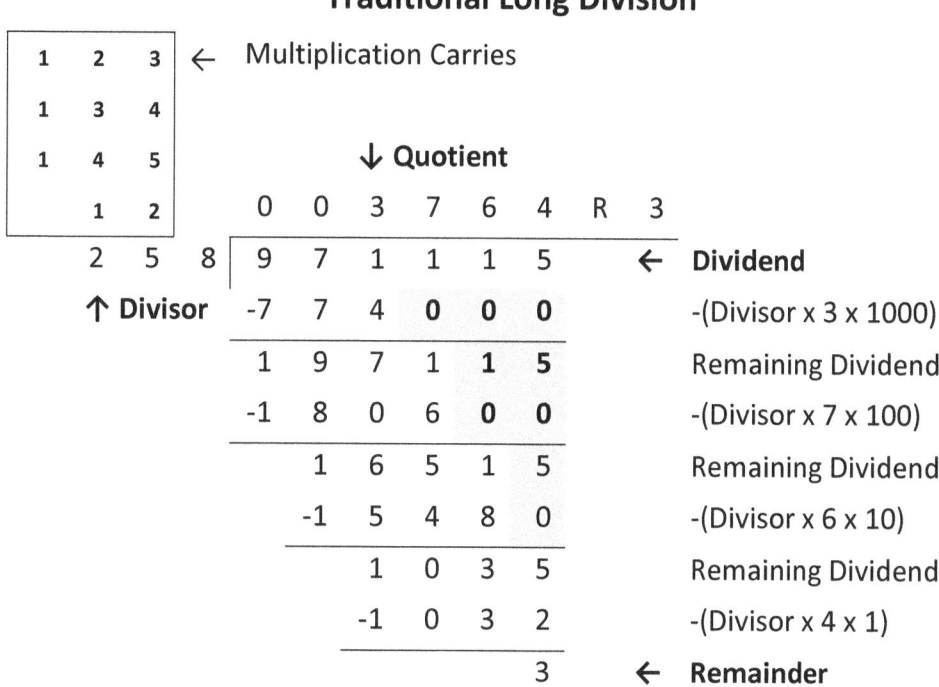

The shaded digits are not written during a traditional long division calculation because they are not used when the digits to their left are used to find quotient digits.

4 Doubling

Doubling a number has the same effect as multiplying the number by two. A number can be quickly doubled by adding the number to itself as described below. Addition carries are indicated by underlining digits as described in step 5a below.

	Number		<u>8</u>	7	<u>2</u>	5	3
	Number Doubled	1	7	4	5	0	6

Doubling is performed as follows:
1. Get the number's right-most (low-order) digit from the top row.
2. Add the digit to itself.
3. If the digit is underlined, add 1 to the sum. (The right-most digit will never be underlined.)
4. Write the units digit of the Step 3 sum below the digit used in Step 2.
5. If the Step 3 sum is greater than 9, do either Step 5a or Step 5b:
    a. If there is another digit to the left of the digit used in Step 2, underline it to show that 1 has been carried to the underlined digit's position or place. Go to Step 6.
    b. If there is no digit to the left of the digit used in Step 2, write"1" in the bottom row one position or place to the left of the digit used in Step 2. Go to Step 7.
6. Get the next digit to left of the digit used in Step 2, then go to Step 2.
7. Stop because the process has ended.

Doubling

A step-by-step example of doubling is shown below.

    8   7   2   5   3   Write the number to be doubled

Then start with the right-most digit and work left, one digit at a time.

	8	7	2	5	**3**	
					6	**3 + 3 = 6**, write **6**.

	8	7	**2**	5	3	
				0	6	**5 + 5 = 10**, write **0** and underline **2** to show that 1 has been carried to this place.

	8	7	**2**	5	3	
			5	0	6	**2** + **2** = 4, 4 + 1 = **5**, write **5**. (The underlined **2** means that 1 was carried to this place.)

	8	7	**2**	5	3	
		4	5	0	6	**7 + 7 = 14**, write **4** and underline **8**.

	8	7	**2**	5	3	**8** + **8** = 16 and 16 + 1 = **17**, write **17**.
1	**7**	4	5	0	6	← 174,506 equals 87,253 doubled.

The figure below shows another step-by-step view of the doubling process.

		8	7	2	5	**3**
						6

		8	7	**2**	5	3
					0	6

		8	7	**2**	5	3
				5	0	6

		8	7	**2**	5	3
			4	5	0	6

		8	7	**2**	5	3
	1	**7**	4	5	0	6

Doubling Examples

	<u>3</u>	9	<u>0</u>	5	2			<u>9</u>	7	<u>0</u>	<u>5</u>	8
	7	8	1	0	4		1	9	4	1	1	6
	<u>6</u>	5	<u>1</u>	<u>6</u>	5			5	0	<u>4</u>	<u>9</u>	5
1	3	0	3	3	0		1	0	0	9	9	0
	<u>1</u>	7	<u>0</u>	<u>5</u>	9			<u>5</u>	9	1	<u>4</u>	6
	3	4	1	1	8		1	1	8	2	9	2
	5	<u>0</u>	6	<u>0</u>	7			<u>4</u>	<u>5</u>	<u>6</u>	<u>7</u>	8
1	0	1	2	1	4			9	1	3	5	6
	<u>5</u>	6	<u>1</u>	<u>5</u>	9			<u>1</u>	<u>6</u>	6	<u>0</u>	8
1	1	2	3	1	8			3	3	2	1	6
	3	4	2	0	1			<u>6</u>	5	<u>1</u>	<u>5</u>	7
	6	8	4	0	2		1	3	0	3	1	4
	<u>9</u>	<u>7</u>	5	<u>0</u>	6			<u>6</u>	5	<u>0</u>	<u>4</u>	9
1	9	5	0	1	2		1	3	0	0	9	8
	4	<u>0</u>	5	<u>3</u>	5			4	<u>0</u>	<u>8</u>	<u>5</u>	6
	8	1	0	7	0			8	1	7	1	2
	<u>9</u>	<u>8</u>	<u>5</u>	<u>6</u>	7			<u>2</u>	9	<u>0</u>	<u>9</u>	7
1	9	7	1	3	4			5	8	1	9	4
	<u>5</u>	<u>5</u>	7	<u>3</u>	9			<u>5</u>	<u>5</u>	5	<u>0</u>	5
1	1	1	4	7	8		1	1	1	0	1	0

Underline digits to indicate borrow activity if it is helpful. However, this technique will not be used later in this book to minimize unnecessary distractions.

5 Table of Multiples

Good News Multiplication and Good News Long Division both use a Table of Multiples that has two columns and five rows. The first column contains the factors 1, 2, 4, 6, and 8. The second column contains multiples of a given base number. The first number in the second column is the given base number, or simply "base," and its factor is 1 because 1 times the base equals the base. Each of the numbers in second column is the product of the base and the corresponding factor in the first column. Multiples of the base for factors 2, 4, and 8 are produced by doubling. The multiple for factor 6 is the sum of the multiple for factor 2 plus the multiple for factor 4. First-column factors are followed by "x" to visually separate them from multiples of the base number in the second column.

The base in the following Table of Multiples is **378**.
Multiples for Factors 2, 4, and 8 are produced by doubling.
Multiple for Factor 6 = Multiple for Factor 2 + Multiple for Factor 6.

Table of Multiples

Factor	Multiple					
1x		**3**	**7**	**8**	Base = **378**	(1 x Base)
2x		7	5	6	378 + 378 = **756**	(2 x Base)
4x	1	5	1	2	756 + 756 = **1512**	(4 x Base)
6x	2	2	6	8	756 + 1512 = **2268**	(6 x Base)
8x	3	0	2	4	1512 + 1512 = **3024**	(8 x Base)

Note: 6 x Base = (2 x Base) + (4 x Base) = 756 + 1512 = 2268

Table of Multiples

Below is a step-by-step example of building a Table of Multiples for the base **378**.

1. Start with the column of factors and the base **378**.

1x		3	7	8
2x				
4x				
6x				
8x				

2. Use doubling to produce the multiples for factors 2, 4, and 8.

   378 + 378 = <u>756</u>   756 + 756 = <u>1512</u>   1512 + 1512 = <u>3024</u>

1x		3	7	8
2x		7	5	6
4x	1	5	1	2
6x				
8x	3	0	2	4

3. Add the multiple for the factor 2 to the multiple for the factor 4 to get the multiple for the factor **6**: 756 + 1512 = **2268**.

1x		3	7	8
2x		7	5	6
4x	1	5	1	2
6x	**2**	**2**	**6**	**8**
8x	3	0	2	4

Note: Two times a number plus four times the number equals six times the number.

Table of Multiples

Checking the Table of Multiples is very important because an error in this table will result in many other errors. The Table of Multiples can be checked in either of two ways: the process that created the table can be repeated, or the method shown below can be used.

The Table of Multiples can be checked as follows:
(6 x Base) + (8 x Base) = 14 x Base
(14 x Base) − (4 x Base) = 10 x Base

Table of Multiples

Factor		Multiple			
1x		3	7	8	← Base
2x		7	5	6	
4x	1	5	1	2	
6x	2	2	6	8	
8x	3	0	2	4	
14x	5	2	9	2	
-4x	-1	5	1	2	
10x	3	7	8	0	← 10 x Base

Check

The base in the Table of Multiples is the multiplicand in Good News Multiplication and the divisor in Good News Long Division.

Please use this method of checking the Table of Multiples if it is helpful. However, it will seldom be used in the examples that follow to minimize unnecessary distractions.

6 Numbers in Expanded Form

A number's expanded form shows that the number is the sum of the products of each of its digits and a power of ten corresponding to the digit's place value in the number.

For example: 5793 = (5 x 1000) + (7 x 100) + (9 x 10) + (3 x 1) = 5000 + 700 + 90 + 3

(Powers of ten: 10^0 = 1; 10^1 = 10; 10^2 = 100; 10^3 = 1000; 10^4 = 10,000; 10^5 = 100,000; 10^6 = 1,000,000; etc.)

> Good News Multiplication uses a ***special expanded form*** of the multiplier where the digits 3, 5, 7, and 9 are replaced by the next smaller even digit plus one:
> **3** = 2 + 1,   **5** = 4 + 1,   **7** = 6 + 1,   and **9** = 8 + 1.

In the figure below, the Traditional Expanded Form of 5793 is written vertically in the left column and totaled to verify the expansion. The corresponding Special Expanded Form is written in the right column and totaled to show that it produces the same total.

	Traditional Expanded Form of **5793**					Special Expanded Form of **5793**			
+	5	0	0	0	+	4	0	0	0
					+	1	0	0	0
+		7	0	0	+		6	0	0
					+		1	0	0
+			9	0	+			8	0
					+			1	0
+				3	+				2
					+				1
	5	7	9	3		5	7	9	3

Note: From now on, the "special expanded form" will simply be called the "expanded form," and the plus signs (+) will not be shown.

Numbers in Expanded Form

The procedure for writing a number in expanded form is as follows:
1. Write the number to be expanded, which will be called the base. Start with the left-most digit of the base and work right, one digit at a time.
2. Do one of the following for each digit of the base:
    a. If the digit is zero, do nothing – move right one place and repeat step 2.
    b. For digits 1, 2, 4, 6, or 8; copy the digit directly beneath itself in a **new row**.
    c. For digits 3, 5, 7, or 9; write the next smaller even digit in a **new row** directly beneath the digit, then write 1 in another **new row** directly beneath this even digit.
3. Count the number of places to the right of the base digit used in Step 2b or 2c.
4. Put the same number of zeros as counted in Step 3 on the right side of the 2b digit or on the right side of both 2c digits.

Step 4 has the effect of multiplying a digit in the base by the power of ten that corresponds to the digit's place value.

Numbers in Expanded Form

In the example below, the base to be expanded is shown in the shaded top row while its non-zero digits are shown in the shaded left column.

	9	2	7	4	0	0	5	6	1	3
9	8	0	0	0	0	0	0	0	0	0
	1	0	0	0	0	0	0	0	0	0
2		2	0	0	0	0	0	0	0	0
7			6	0	0	0	0	0	0	0
			1	0	0	0	0	0	0	0
4				4	0	0	0	0	0	0
5							4	0	0	0
							1	0	0	0
6								6	0	0
1									1	0
3										2
										1
	9	2	7	4	0	0	5	6	1	3

Expanded-form rows are not created for zeros in the base.

Expanded Form Examples

The numbers to be expanded are shown in the shaded areas with their expanded forms shown directly beneath them. The expanded-form rows are totaled to verify the expansions. Each shaded number equals the total of the expanded-form rows under it.

	1	**0**	**2**	**3**
	1	0	0	0
		2	0	
			2	
				1
	1	0	2	3

	3	**2**	**0**	**1**
	2	0	0	0
	1	0	0	0
		2	0	0
				1
	3	2	0	1

	5	**6**	**7**	**8**
	4	0	0	0
	1	0	0	0
		6	0	0
			6	0
			1	0
				8
	5	6	7	8

8	**7**	**6**	**5**	**0**
8	0	0	0	0
	6	0	0	0
	1	0	0	0
		6	0	0
			4	0
			1	0
8	7	6	5	0

9	**0**	**0**	**0**
8	0	0	0
1	0	0	0
9	0	0	0

1	**0**	**2**	**0**
1	0	0	0
		2	0
1	0	2	0

9	**0**	**0**	**3**
8	0	0	0
1	0	0	0
			2
			1
9	0	0	3

3	**1**	**5**	**7**	**9**
2	0	0	0	0
1	0	0	0	0
	1	0	0	0
		4	0	0
		1	0	0
			6	0
			1	0
				8
				1
3	1	5	7	9

Expanded Form Examples

Totals for the expanded rows are not shown below because these totals are usually not written when using Good News Multiplication. Nevertheless, always verify that the sum of the expanded-form rows equals the number expanded.

1	2	3	4	5
1	0	0	0	0
	2	0	0	0
		2	0	0
		1	0	0
			4	0
				4
				1

2	0	1	6	8
2	0	0	0	0
		1	0	0
			6	0
				8

8	0	1	0	0	0	4	5
8	0	0	0	0	0	0	0
		1	0	0	0	0	0
						4	0
							4
							1

3	3	3	3
2	0	0	0
1	0	0	0
	2	0	0
	1	0	0
		2	0
		1	0
			2
			1

9	2	0	0	7	5
8	0	0	0	0	0
1	0	0	0	0	0
	2	0	0	0	0
				6	0
				1	0
					4
					1

3	5	7	9	2	4	6	8
2	0	0	0	0	0	0	0
1	0	0	0	0	0	0	0
	4	0	0	0	0	0	0
	1	0	0	0	0	0	0
		6	0	0	0	0	0
		1	0	0	0	0	0
			8	0	0	0	0
			1	0	0	0	0
				2	0	0	0
					4	0	0
						6	0
							8

1	0	0	0	4	7	0	0	0
1	0	0	0	0	0	0	0	0
				4	0	0	0	0
					6	0	0	0
					1	0	0	0

7 Short Division

Short division may be the most efficient division method for divisors 2 - 12.

Divide 16,059 by 9

```
    0   1   7   8   4   R 3
  ┌─────────────────────────
9 │ 1  ¹6  ⁷0  ⁷5  ³9
```

Step-by-step Example of Short Division

Work through the dividend from left to right, one digit at a time. Write each division remainder above and to the left of the next dividend digit with which it is now linked to make a two digit number. For example: **1** linked to **6** is $^1 6$ = **16** = (**1** x **10**) + **6**.

9 │ 1 6 0 5 9	Write problem in standard form. Leave space above and between dividend digits. "R" stands for "remainder" in instructions below.
0 9 │ 1 ¹6 0 5 9	1 ÷ 9 = 0 with R = 1. Write 0 in quotient. Link R to next dividend digit 6 to make $^1 6$ = 16.
0 1 9 │ 1 ¹6 ⁷0 5 9	$^1 6$ ÷ 9 = 1 with R = 7. Write 1 in quotient. Link R to next dividend digit 0 to make $^7 0$ = 70.
0 1 7 9 │ 1 ¹6 ⁷0 ⁷5 9	$^7 0$ ÷ 9 = 7 with R = 7. Write 7 in quotient. Link R to next dividend digit 5 to make $^7 5$ = 75.
0 1 7 8 9 │ 1 ¹6 ⁷0 ⁷5 ³9	$^7 5$ ÷ 9 = 8 with R = 3. Write 8 in quotient. Link R to next dividend digit 9 to make $^3 9$ = 39.
0 1 7 8 4 R 3 9 │ 1 ¹6 ⁷0 ⁷5 ³9	$^3 9$ ÷ 9 = 4 with R = 3. Write 4 in quotient and "R 3" next to it because no more dividend digits remain to right of $^3 9$.

Quotient = 1,784 with **Remainder = 3**

Short Division Examples

```
      3  3  0  2  3 R 1              0  5  0   5   5  4
2 | 6  6  0  4  7              2 | 1 ¹0  1  ¹1  ¹0  8


      2  2  0  1   5 R 2             3  0   7   6   9   5 R 2
3 | 6  6  0  4  ¹7             3 | 9  2  ²3  ²0  ²8  ¹7


      1  6   5  1  1 R 3             0   2   5   4   5   6 R 1
4 | 6 ²6  ²0  4  7              4 | 1 ¹0  ²1  ¹8  ²2  ²5


      1  3   2  0   9 R 2            1   2  1   2   7  0
5 | 6 ¹6  ¹0  4  ⁴7             5 | 6 ¹0  6  ¹3  ³5  0


      1  1  0  0   7 R 5             0   3   4   9   7  1
6 | 6  6  0  4  ⁴7             6 | 2 ²0  ²9  ⁵8  ⁴2  6


      0  9   4   3   5 R 2           1   4   1   5  0   5
7 | 6 ⁶6  ³0  ²4  ³7            7 | 9 ²9  ¹0  ³5  3  ³5


      0  8   2   5   5 R 7           0   7   9   3   7   7 R 6
8 | 6 ⁶6  ²0  ⁴4  ⁴7            8 | 6 ⁶3  ⁷5  ³0  ⁶2  ⁶2
```

Note: "R 0" is usually not written when the remainder is zero.

Short Division Examples

```
      0   7   3   3   8  R 5              0   1   1   1   2   2
  9 | 6  ⁶6  ³0  ³4  ⁷7                9 | 1  ¹0  ¹0  ¹0  ¹9  ¹8


      0   6   6   0   4  R 7              0   1   8   4   0   0  R 9
 10 | 6  ⁶6  ⁶0   4  ⁴7               10 | 1  ¹8  ⁸4  ⁴0   0   9


      0   6   0   0   4  R 3              0   8   7   1   2   8
 11 | 6  ⁶6   0   4  ⁴7               11 | 9  ⁹5  ⁷8  ¹4  ³0  ⁸8


      0   5   5   0   3  R11              0   0   9   9   1   6  R 8
 12 | 6  ⁶6  ⁶0   4  ⁴7               12 | 1  ¹1  ¹¹9 ¹¹0 ²0  ⁸0


      1   0   0   9   7   1   3   3   3   7   2   3   5   6  R 5
  9 | 9   0   8  ⁸7  ⁶4  ¹2  ³0  ³0  ³3  ⁶5  ²1  ³2  ⁵0  ⁵9


      0   0   8   3   5   8   8   1   6   0   0   9   5   6  R10
 12 | 1  ¹0  ¹⁰0  ⁴3  ⁷0  ¹⁰5 ⁹7  ¹9  ⁷2   1  ¹1  ¹¹4  ⁶8  ⁸2
```

Note: Leading zeros in whole numbers do not have a non-zero digit to their left. Leading zeros contribute no value to a number and do not need to be written. However, leading zeros have been written in the examples above to maintain alignment, avoid place errors, and emphasize the fact that **each dividend digit produces a quotient digit**, even if it is only a leading zero.

8 Good News Multiplication

Good News Multiplication uses a table of multiplicand multiples and the expanded form of the multiplier. Good News Multiplication emphasizes the fact that multiplication is repeated addition.

Good News Multiplication is performed as follows:
1. Write the problem in horizontal form: multiplicand x multiplier.
2. Put a table of multiplicand multiples under the multiplicand.
3. Put the expanded form of the multiplier under the multiplier.
4. For each row of in the expanded multiplier column, do the following:
    a. Match the row's first digit with a factor in the table of multiplicand multiples and get the corresponding multiple.
    b. Count the row's zeros and put this many zeros on the right side of the multiplicand multiple from 4a to make a partial product.
    c. Copy this partial product to a right-justified column.
5. The sum of the partial products' column equals the final product of the multiplication.

The effect of Step 4b is to multiply the multiplicand multiple by the power of ten that corresponds to the place value of the multiplier digit.

Note: The numbers in a right-justified column are aligned so that the right-most (low-order) digits of these numbers form a vertical column.

Good News Multiplication Example

The following step-by-step example shows how to use Good News Multiplication to multiplying 378 by 271. Each numbered instruction is followed by a figure that shows what needs to be done.

1. Write the problem in horizontal form.

    3 7 8 x 2 7 1

2. Build the table of multiplicand multiples.
    a. Write the factors 1, 2, 4, 6, and 8 followed by "x."
    b. Calculate multiples of the multiplicand **378** for factors 2, 4, and 8 as follows:
       378 + 378 = **756**, 756 + 756 = **1512**, 1512 = 1512 = **3024**
    c. Then calculate the multiple for the factor 6 as follows:
       756 + 1512 = **2268**

1x			3	7	8	x	2	7	1
2x				7	5	6			
4x		1	5	1	2				
6x		2	2	6	8				
8x		3	0	2	4				

    <u>Warning</u>: Be sure to check the table of multiplicand multiples before proceeding.

3. Expand the multiplier **271** beneath itself.

1x			3	7	8	x	2	7	1
2x				7	5	6	2	0	0
4x		1	5	1	2			6	0
6x		2	2	6	8			1	0
8x		3	0	2	4				1

    Verify that the sum of the expanded form rows equals the multiplier:
    200 + 60 + 10 + 1 = **271**.

Good News Multiplication Example

4. Start with the first row of the expanded multiplier. Match this row's first digit **2** with the factor **2** in the table of multiplicand multiples. The multiple for this factor is 756. Copy 756 two spaces to the right of 200, and then put the two zeros from 200 on the right side of 756. This first partial product of 75600 will be the alignment guide for partial products that follow.

1x			3	7	8	x	2	7	1				
2x				7	5	6	**2**	**0**	**0**		7	5	6	**0**	**0**
4x		1	5	1	2		6	0					
6x		2	2	6	8		1	0					
8x		3	0	2	4			1					

5. Move down to the next row of the expanded multiplier. The first digit of this row is 6.

   a. Copy the **0** following 6 to the low-order position of the partial products' column.

1x			3	7	8	x	2	7	1				
2x				7	5	6	2	0	0		7	5	6	0	0
4x		1	5	1	2		**6**	**0**						**0**
6x		2	2	6	8		1	0					
8x		3	0	2	4			1					

Good News Multiplication Example

    b. Copy multiple 2268 corresponding to factor **6** to the partial products' column. (Write the digits 2268 in **right to left** order to keep them properly aligned: write the 8 first and then 6, 2, and 2.)

```
1x              3 7 8    x  2 7 1
2x              7 5 6       2 0 0         7 5 6 0 0
4x          1   5 1 2         6 0         2 2 6 8 0
6x          2   2 6 8         1 0
8x          3   0 2 4           1
```

Note: This two-step process (5a and 5b above) for writing partial products after the first one helps keep the partial products properly aligned and right justified.

6. Move down to the next row of the expanded multiplier. This row's first digit is **1**. Copy the **0** following this **1** to the low-order position of the partial products' column and then copy the multiple for the factor **1** in front of this **0**.

```
1x              3 7 8    x  2 7 1
2x              7 5 6       2 0 0         7 5 6 0 0
4x          1   5 1 2         6 0         2 2 6 8 0
6x          2   2 6 8         1 0           3 7 8 0
8x          3   0 2 4           1
```

Good News Multiplication Example

7. Move down to the last row of the expanded multiplier. Copy the multiple for the factor **1** to the last row of the partial products' column so that it is right justified.

					x	2	7	1					
1x			3	7	8								
2x			7	5	6		2	0	0		7	5	6	0	0
4x		1	5	1	2			6	0		2	2	6	8	0
6x		2	2	6	8			1	0			3	7	8	0
8x		3	0	2	4				1				3	7	8

Total the partial products' column to get 102,438 = 378 x 271.

					x	2	7	1			*1*	*2*	*2*		
1x			3	7	8										
2x			7	5	6		2	0	0		7	5	6	0	0
4x		1	5	1	2			6	0		2	2	6	8	0
6x		2	2	6	8			1	0			3	7	8	0
8x		3	0	2	4				1				3	7	8
										1	0	2	4	3	8

Note: The digits *1 2 2* in the top row of the right column are addition carry values.

The figure above is shown below without shading.

					x	2	7	1			*1*	*2*	*2*		
1x			3	7	8										
2x			7	5	6		2	0	0		7	5	6	0	0
4x		1	5	1	2			6	0		2	2	6	8	0
6x		2	2	6	8			1	0			3	7	8	0
8x		3	0	2	4				1				3	7	8
										1	0	2	4	3	8

378 x 271 = 102,438

9 Multiplication Examples

Good News Multiplication examples are shown below. These examples show how the calculations look using grid paper, which helps maintain proper column alignment.

Summary
- Match the left-most digit of each expanded-multiplier row with a factor in table of multiplicand multiples. • Get the corresponding multiple. • Copy the expanded-multiplier row's zeros onto right side of this multiple to form a partial product.
- Sum the partial products to get the product of the multiplication.

Single-digit Multipliers

Traditional multiplication works well with single-digit multipliers. However, it requires accurate recall of the basic multiplication tables and some error-prone mental math. Good News Multiplication involves no multiplication and very little mental math.

```
1x              9 x 8
2x      1 8       8        7 2
4x      3 6
6x      5 4
8x      7 2


1x              7 x 9
2x      1 4       8       5 6
4x      2 8       1         7
6x      4 2                6 3
8x      5 6


1x             4 5 x 4
2x       9 0     4       1 8 0
4x     1 8 0
6x     2 7 0
8x     3 6 0
```

35

Single-digit Multipliers

1x			**5**	**9**	**x**	**7**					
2x		1	1	8		6		3	5	4	
4x		2	3	6		1			5	9	
6x		3	5	4				**4**	**1**	**3**	
8x		4	7	2							

1x			**2**	**3**	**4**	**x**	**4**				
2x			4	6	8		4		**1**	**4**	**0**	**4**
4x			9	3	6						
6x		1	4	0	4						
8x		1	8	7	2						

1x			**5**	**4**	**5**	**5**	**x**	**9**				
2x		1	0	9	1	0		8		4	3	6	4	0
4x		2	1	8	2	0		1			5	4	5	5
6x		3	2	7	3	0				**4**	**9**	**0**	**9**	**5**
8x		4	3	6	4	0						

1x			**2**	**4**	**7**	**9**	**x**	**5**				
2x			4	9	5	8		4		9	9	1	6
4x			9	9	1	6		1		2	4	7	9
6x		1	4	8	7	4			**1**	**2**	**3**	**9**	**5**
8x		1	9	8	3	2						

1x			**7**	**8**	**6**	**4**	**x**	**9**				
2x		1	5	7	2	8		8		6	2	9	1	2
4x		3	1	4	5	6		1			7	8	6	4
6x		4	7	1	8	4				**7**	**0**	**7**	**7**	**6**
8x		6	2	9	1	2						

Single-digit Multipliers

In the example below, the expanded form of the multiplier has been copied to a new location where there is more space to write the partial products.

```
1x           3 4 5 6 7 8 0 1  x  9
2x           6 9 1 3 5 6 0 2     8
4x         1 3 8 2 7 1 2 0 4     1
6x         2 0 7 4 0 6 8 0 6
8x         2 7 6 5 4 2 4 0 8

           8     2 7 6 5 4 2 4 0 8
           1       3 4 5 6 7 8 0 1
                 3 1 1 1 1 0 2 0 9
```

```
1x         4 5 0 0 9 8 5 7 6 3 5  x  7
2x         9 0 0 1 9 7 1 5 2 7 0     6
4x       1 8 0 0 3 9 4 3 0 5 4 0     1
6x       2 7 0 0 5 9 1 4 5 8 1 0
8x       3 6 0 0 7 8 8 6 1 0 8 0

6          2 7 0 0 5 9 1 4 5 8 1 0
1            4 5 0 0 9 8 5 7 6 3 5
           3 1 5 0 6 9 0 0 3 4 4 5
↑                                ↑
Expanded Multiplier              Product
```

Two-digit Multipliers

1x		1	9	x	1	7			*1*	*1*	
2x		3	8		1	0			1	9	0
4x		7	6			6			1	1	4
6x	1	1	4			1				1	9
8x	1	5	2						**3**	**2**	**3**
1x		3	5	x	2	9			*1*		
2x		7	0		2	0			7	0	0
4x	1	4	0			8			2	8	0
6x	2	1	0			1				3	5
8x	2	8	0					**1**	**0**	**1**	**5**
1x		7	5	x	6	3			*1*		
2x	1	5	0		6	0		4	5	0	0
4x	3	0	0			2			1	5	0
6x	4	5	0			1				7	5
8x	6	0	0						**4**	**7**	**2**	**5**
1x		8	4	x	6	2			*1*		
2x	1	6	8		6	0		5	0	4	0
4x	3	3	6			2			1	6	8
6x	5	0	4					**5**	**2**	**0**	**8**
8x	6	7	2								

Place-holder zeros are shaded to distinguish them from the low-order digits of the multiplicand multiples.

Two-digit Multipliers

					×							
1×			5	9	×	3	7		*1*	*2*	*1*	
2×		1	1	8		2	0		1	1	8	0
4×		2	3	6		1	0			5	9	0
6×		3	5	4			6			3	5	4
8×		4	7	2			1				5	9
									2	**1**	**8**	**3**

1×			8	0	×	5	9		*1*	*1*		
2×		1	6	0		4	0		3	2	0	0
4×		3	2	0		1	0			8	0	0
6×		4	8	0			8			6	4	0
8×		6	4	0			1				8	0
									4	**7**	**2**	**0**

1×			3	1	7	×	9	5		*1*	*1*	*2*	*1*	
2×			6	3	4		8	0		2	5	3	6	0
4×		1	2	6	8		1	0			3	1	7	0
6×		1	9	0	2			4			1	2	6	8
8×		2	5	3	6			1				3	1	7
										3	**0**	**1**	**1**	**5**

1×			2	4	7	5	9	×	7	5		*2*	*2*	*1*	*2*	*1*	
2×			4	9	5	1	8		6	0		1	4	8	5	5	4	0
4×			9	9	0	3	6		1	0			2	4	7	5	9	0
6×		1	4	8	5	5	4			4				9	9	0	3	6
8×		1	9	8	0	7	2			1					2	4	7	5	9
													1	**8**	**5**	**6**	**9**	**2**	**5**

Three-digit Multipliers

1x			2	5	6	x	1	2	3			*1*	*1*		
2x			5	1	2			1	0	0		2	5	6	0	0
4x		1	0	2	4			2	0				5	1	2	0
6x		1	5	3	6				2					5	1	2
8x		2	0	4	8				1					2	5	6
												3	1	4	8	8

1x			9	4	7	x	9	0	0	*1*	*1*	*1*		
2x		1	8	9	4		8	0	0	7	5	7	6	0	0
4x		3	7	8	8		1	0	0		9	4	7	0	0
6x		5	6	8	2					8	5	2	3	0	0
8x		7	5	7	6										

1x			9	4	7	x	7	4	0	*2*	*2*	*1*		
2x		1	8	9	4		6	0	0	5	6	8	2	0	0
4x		3	7	8	8		1	0	0		9	4	7	0	0
6x		5	6	8	2			4	0		3	7	8	8	0
8x		7	5	7	6					7	0	0	7	8	0

1x			9	4	7	x	2	6	8	*1*	*2*	*1*		
2x		1	8	9	4		2	0	0	1	8	9	4	0	0
4x		3	7	8	8			6	0		5	6	8	2	0
6x		5	6	8	2				8			7	5	7	6
8x		7	5	7	6					2	5	3	7	9	6

1x			9	4	7	x	6	6	6	*1*	*2*	*1*	*1*	
2x		1	8	9	4		6	0	0	5	6	8	2	0	0
4x		3	7	8	8		6	0			5	6	8	2	0
6x		5	6	8	2			6				5	6	8	2
8x		7	5	7	6					6	3	0	7	0	2

Three-digit Multipliers

Gridlines are not used in the following examples to make it easier to see how the partial products are formed. Place-holder zeros are shaded.

```
1x           9 4 7  x  3 0 5           1 1 2 1 1
2x       1 8 9 4       2 0 0         1 8 9 4 0 0
4x       3 7 8 8       1 0 0             9 4 7 0 0
6x       5 6 8 2           4                 3 7 8 8
8x       7 5 7 6           1                     9 4 7
                                     ─────────────────
                                     2 8 8 8 3 5
```

```
1x           9 4 7  x  5 3 7           2 3 4 2
2x       1 8 9 4       4 0 0         3 7 8 8 0 0
4x       3 7 8 8       1 0 0             9 4 7 0 0
6x       5 6 8 2           2 0           1 8 9 4 0
8x       7 5 7 6           1 0               9 4 7 0
                           6                 5 6 8 2
                           1                     9 4 7
                                     ─────────────────
                                     5 0 8 5 3 9
```

```
1x           9 4 7  x  1 5 9           3 3 2 1
2x       1 8 9 4       1 0 0             9 4 7 0 0
4x       3 7 8 8           4 0           3 7 8 8 0
6x       5 6 8 2           1 0               9 4 7 0
8x       7 5 7 6           8                 7 5 7 6
                           1                     9 4 7
                                     ─────────────────
                                     1 5 0 5 7 3
```

```
1x           9 4 7  x  7 9 5           2 3 3 2 1
2x       1 8 9 4       6 0 0         5 6 8 2 0 0
4x       3 7 8 8       1 0 0             9 4 7 0 0
6x       5 6 8 2           8 0           7 5 7 6 0
8x       7 5 7 6           1 0               9 4 7 0
                           4                 3 7 8 8
                           1                     9 4 7
                                     ─────────────────
                                     7 5 2 8 6 5
```

Three-digit Multipliers

```
1x      1 3 4 6 8  x  3 6 5           1 2 2 2 2 1
2x      2 6 9 3 6     2 0 0           2 6 9 3 6 0 0
4x      5 3 8 7 2     1 0 0           1 3 4 6 8 0 0
6x      8 0 8 0 8         6 0             8 0 8 0 8 0
8x    1 0 7 7 4 4           4             5 3 8 7 2
                            1               1 3 4 6 8
                                      4 9 1 5 8 2 0


1x      1 3 4 6 8  x  7 9 3             2 3 4 2 1
2x      2 6 9 3 6     6 0 0           8 0 8 0 8 0 0
4x      5 3 8 7 2     1 0 0           1 3 4 6 8 0 0
6x      8 0 8 0 8         8 0         1 0 7 7 4 4 0
8x    1 0 7 7 4 4         1 0           1 3 4 6 8 0
                            2             2 6 9 3 6
                            1               1 3 4 6 8
                                    1 0 6 8 0 1 2 4
```

Four-digit Multipliers

```
1x        8 7 5 2 1 4    x  3 7 9 5
2x      1 7 5 0 4 2 8       Multiplier ↑
4x      3 5 0 0 8 5 6
─────────────────────
6x      5 2 5 1 2 8 4
8x      7 0 0 1 7 1 2
```

Expanded Multiplier												
	2	0	0	0		2	3	3	3	2	3	2	1	1

```
Expanded Multiplier          2 3 3 3 2 3 2 1 1
         2 0 0 0           1 7 5 0 4 2 8 0 0 0
         1 0 0 0             8 7 5 2 1 4 0 0 0
           6 0 0             5 2 5 1 2 8 4 0 0
           1 0 0               8 7 5 2 1 4 0 0
             8 0               7 0 0 1 7 1 2 0
             1 0                 8 7 5 2 1 4 0
               4                 3 5 0 0 8 5 6
               1                   8 7 5 2 1 4
        ──────────        ───────────────────────
         3 7 9 5           3 3 2 1 4 3 7 1 3 0
```

```
1x        8 7 5 2 1 4    x  8 0 1 5
2x      1 7 5 0 4 2 8       ↑ Multiplier
4x      3 5 0 0 8 5 6
─────────────────────
6x      5 2 5 1 2 8 4
8x      7 0 0 1 7 1 2
```

```
Expanded Multiplier                1 2   1 1 1 1
         8 0 0 0           7 0 0 1 7 1 2 0 0 0
             1 0               8 7 5 2 1 4 0
              4                3 5 0 0 8 5 6
              1                  8 7 5 2 1 4
        ──────────        ───────────────────────
         8 0 1 5           │7 0 1 4 8 4 0 2 1 0│
```

Note: The expanded multiplier rows are totaled in the above example because they do not lie directly under the multiplier for easy visual verification.

Five-digit Multipliers

```
1x        4  8  7  6  5  0  3    x  7  3  8  5  6
2x        9  7  5  3  0  0  6       Multiplier ↑
4x     1  9  5  0  6  0  1  2
6x     2  9  2  5  9  0  1  8
8x     3  9  0  1  2  0  2  4
```

```
   Expanded Multiplier              1  3  4  4  3  2  3  2
      6  0  0  0  0              2  9  2  5  9  0  1  8  0  0  0  0
      1  0  0  0  0                 4  8  7  6  5  0  3  0  0  0  0
         2  0  0  0                    9  7  5  3  0  0  6  0  0  0
         1  0  0  0                       4  8  7  6  5  0  3  0  0
            8  0  0                          3  9  0  1  2  0  2  4  0  0
               4  0                             1  9  5  0  6  0  1  2  0
               1  0                                4  8  7  6  5  0  3  0
                  6                                   2  9  2  5  9  0  1  8
      ─────────────                  ───────────────────────────────────────
      7  3  8  5  6                  3  6  0  1  5  9  0  0  5  5  6  8
```

```
1x        3  7  8  6  5    x  5  7  0  0  3  9
2x        7  5  7  3  0       Multiplier ↑
4x     1  5  1  4  6  0
6x     2  2  7  1  9  0
8x     3  0  2  9  2  0
```

```
   Expanded Multiplier              1  1  2  2  3  2  2  2  1
   4  0  0  0  0  0              1  5  1  4  6  0  0  0  0  0  0
   1  0  0  0  0  0                 3  7  8  6  5  0  0  0  0  0
      6  0  0  0  0                 2  2  7  1  9  0  0  0  0  0
      1  0  0  0  0                    3  7  8  6  5  0  0  0  0
         2  0  0  0                          7  5  7  3  0  0
         1  0  0  0                          3  7  8  6  5  0
            8  0  0                          3  0  2  9  2  0
               1                                3  7  8  6  5
   ──────────────────               ───────────────────────────────
   5  7  0  0  3  9                  2  1  5  8  4  5  2  6  7  3  5
```

Final Multiplication Example

The example below shows the power of Good News Multiplication. Correctly adding the columns of digits in the partial products is the most difficult part of the task.

				↓ Multiplicand							x	7	3	↓ Multiplier 9	7	0	9	0	5
1x				9	8	7	6	5	4	3	2	1						
2x			1	9	7	5	3	0	8	6	4	2						
4x			3	9	5	0	6	1	7	2	8	4						
6x			5	9	2	5	9	2	5	9	2	6						
8x			7	9	0	1	2	3	4	5	6	8						

Expanded Multiplier:

```
6 0 0 0 0 0 0 0
1 0 0 0 0 0 0 0
  2 0 0 0 0 0 0
  1 0 0 0 0 0 0
    8 0 0 0 0 0
    1 0 0 0 0 0
      6 0 0 0 0
      1 0 0 0 0
        8 0 0
        1 0 0
          4
          1
```

← Expanded Multiplier

The shaded areas are place-holder zeros.

The row above the partial products below are addition carries.

	2	4	5	5	4	5	6	5	5	4	3	2	1	2		
	5	9	2	5	9	2	5	9	2	6	0	0	0	0	0	0
		9	8	7	6	5	4	3	2	1	0	0	0	0	0	0
		1	9	7	5	3	0	8	6	4	2	0	0	0	0	0
			9	8	7	6	5	4	3	2	1	0	0	0	0	0
			7	9	0	1	2	3	4	5	6	8	0	0	0	0
				9	8	7	6	5	4	3	2	1	0	0	0	0
				5	9	2	5	9	2	5	9	2	6	0	0	0
					9	8	7	6	5	4	3	2	1	0	0	0
					7	9	0	1	2	3	4	5	6	8	0	0
						9	8	7	6	5	4	3	2	1	0	0
Product|							5	9	2	5	9	2	5	9	2	6
↓									9	8	7	6	5	4	3	2	1
	7	3	0	5	7	6	8	5	9	2	6	8	3	9	1	4	7

10 Good News Long Division

Given a dividend and a divisor, make a Table of Multiples for the divisor, then repeat the steps below until the remaining dividend is less than the divisor. The initial remaining dividend is the given dividend.

1. Find smallest series of high-order digits in remaining dividend such that number formed from these digits is greater than or equal to divisor.
2. Find largest multiple in Table of Multiples that does not exceed step-1 number. Factor in Table of Multiples that corresponds to this multiple is quotient digit. Its place value is same as last dividend digit used to make step-1 number.
3. Subtract multiple found in step 2 from step-1 number. If this difference is greater than or equal to divisor, subtract divisor from this difference to get new difference, and increase step-2 quotient digit by one.
4. Make next remaining dividend by appending final step-3 difference in front of dividend digits that are to right of last dividend digit used to make step-1 number.

The quotient equals the sum of the products of the quotient digits and their place values. The remainder is the final step-4 difference.

Good News Long Division's Table of Multiples obviates traditional long division's need for estimating of quotient digits and all multiplication. Section 5 tells how to make a table of multiplies for any base number.

The figure on the next page shows an example of Good News Long Division that matches the description above and shows what actually occurs when the following "Good News Long Division Procedure" is executed.

Good News Long Division

						↓	Quotient	↓				
Table of Divisor							5	7				
↓ Multiples ↓			0	0	8	1	0	4	6	R	2	
1x		3	8	3	0	8	0	1	6	8		← Dividend
2x		7	6	-3	0	4	0	0	0	0		−(8 x Divisor x 10,000)
4x	1	5	2			4	0	1	6	8		← Remaining Dividend
6x	2	2	8			-3	8	0	0	0		−(1 x Divisor x 1000)
8x	3	0	4				2	1	6	8		← Remaining Dividend
							-1	5	2	0		−(4 x Divisor x 10)
								6	4	8		← Remaining Dividend
								-3	8	0		−(1 x Divisor x 10)
								2	6	8		← Remaining Dividend
								-2	2	8		−(6 x Divisor x 1)
									4	0		← Remaining Dividend
									-3	8		−(1 x Divisor x 1)
										2		← Remainder

Quotient 81,057 with Remainder 2

The shaded digits are not written during calculation because they are not used when the digits to their left are used to find quotient digits.

The place value of each quotient digit is the same as the place value of the dividend digit directly under it. This dividend digit is also the dividend digit that terminates the series of high-order digits from the remaining dividend that forms the number that equals or exceeds the divisor.

The first subtraction removes 3,040,000 from the dividend; the remaining dividend after this subtraction is 40,168. In other words, 8 x 10,000 = 80,000 divisor-sized groups are removed from the dividend. The next subtraction effectively removes 1,000 divisor-sized groups from the remaining dividend. This process continues until the remaining dividend is less than the devisor.

Good News Long Division Procedure

Good News Long Division generates a quotient digit for each dividend digit. The procedure is performed as follows:

1. Write the problem in horizontal form.
2. Construct a table of divisor multiples under the divisor.
3. Start with the left-most dividend digit and work right, one digit at a time. Let D be the divisor. Corresponding to each dividend digit is a quotient digit that is written above it.
4. Get the left-most (high-order) dividend digit, and set R equal to this digit.
5. If R < D, the quotient digit is 0. Write 0 above the last digit gotten from the dividend.
6. If R ≥ D, find the largest multiple in the table of divisor multiples such that this multiple does not exceed R. Subtract this multiple from R, and then set R equal to this difference. The quotient digit is the factor in the table of divisor multiples that corresponds to the subtracted multiple. Write this factor above the last digit gotten from the dividend.
7. If R ≥ D after Step 6, subtract D from R, set R equal to this difference, and add 1 to the Step 6 quotient digit. (Step 7 is needed for quotient digits 3, 5, 7, and 9.)
8. If there are more unused dividend digits, get the next one and set T = 10 x R plus this next dividend digit. Next, set R = T and go to step 5 above.
9. If there are no more unused dividend digits, the process ends with the string of quotient digits produced and a remainder equal to the final value of R.

The variables R and T help explain the division process, but are not used in actual calculations.

Attaching the next dividend digit to the right side of R is the same as multiplying R by 10 and adding the next dividend digit. For example, attaching 6 to the right side of 23 produces 236 = (23 x 10) + 6.

Note: Some of the first quotient digits generated may be leading zeros.

Good News Long Division Example 1

The following step-by-step example shows how to use Good News Long Division to divide 3,080,168 by 38. Each numbered instruction is followed by a figure that shows what needs to be done.

1. Write problem in standard form.

$$3\ 8\ |\ 3\ 0\ 8\ 0\ 1\ 6\ 8$$

2. Write the factors 1, 2, 4, 6, and 8 followed by "x" in a column to the left of the divisor.

```
1x           3  8 | 3  0  8  0  1  6  8
2x
4x
6x
8x
```

3. Calculate divisor multiples for factors 2, 4, and 8 by doubling.

38 + 38 = **76**   76 + 76 = **152**   152 + 152 = **304**

```
1x                 3  8 | 3  0  8  0  1  6  8
2x           7  6
4x        1  5  2
6x
8x        3  0  4
```

Good News Long Division Example 1

4. Calculate divisor multiple for factor 6 by addition: 76 + 152 = <u>228</u>.

<u>Table of Divisor Multiples</u>
Factor	Multiple
1x	3 8
2x	7 6
4x	1 5 2
6x	2 2 8
8x	3 0 4

Dividend: 3 8 | 3 0 8 0 1 6 8

The **Table of Divisor Multiples** has a column of single-digit **Factors** on the left and a column of **Multiples** on the right. Each Multiple is the product of the Factor on its left and the Divisor. The "x" separates the Factor from its Multiple.

Warning: Check the table of divisor multiples before proceeding.

5. Start with the first dividend digit on the left and work right, one digit at a time. Since first dividend digit is less than divisor (3 < 38), first quotient digit is 0.

```
                              0
1x          3  8 | 3  0  8  0  1  6  8
2x          7  6
4x       1  5  2
6x       2  2  8
8x       3  0  4
```

6. Since 3 < divisor, link first two dividend digits to make 30. Since 30 < divisor, second quotient digit is 0.

```
                           0  0
1x          3  8 | 3  0  8  0  1  6  8
2x          7  6
4x       1  5  2
6x       2  2  8
8x       3  0  4
```

Good News Long Division Example 1

7. Since 30 < divisor, link first three dividend digits to make 308.
   Since 308 ≥ divisor, find largest divisor multiple that is not larger than 308.
   This multiple is **304**, so third quotient digit is factor **8** corresponding to **304**.

   ```
                          0  0  8
   1x          3  8 | 3  0  8  0  1  6  8
   2x          7  6
   4x       1  5  2
   6x       2  2  8
   8x       3  0  4
   ```

8. Subtract 304 from 308 to get **4**.

   ```
                          0  0  8
   1x          3  8 | 3  0  8  0  1  6  8
   2x          7  6  -3  0  4
   4x       1  5  2            4
   6x       2  2  8
   8x       3  0  4
   ```

Warning: Check each subtraction immediately after it is done by adding the subtrahend to the difference to get the minuend. This check eliminates most errors. In the example above, **verify that 304 + 4 = 308**.

Good News Long Division Example 1

9. Since 4 < divisor, link 4 to next dividend digit to make 40.
   Since 40 ≥ divisor, find largest divisor multiple that is not larger than 40.
   This multiple is **38**, so fourth quotient digit is factor **1** corresponding to **38**.

					0	0	8	1		
1x			3	8	3	0	8	0	1	6	8
2x			7	6	-3	0	4			
4x	1	5	2				4	0		
6x	2	2	8							
8x	3	0	4							

10. Subtract 38 from 40 to get **2**.

					0	0	8	1		
1x			3	8	3	0	8	0	1	6	8
2x			7	6	-3	0	4			
4x	1	5	2				4	0		
6x	2	2	8				-3	8		
8x	3	0	4					2		

Good News Long Division Example 1

11. Since 2 < divisor, link 2 to next dividend digit to make 21.
    Since 21 < divisor, fifth quotient digit is 0.

							0	0	8	1	0		
1x				3	8	|	3	0	8	0	1	6	7
2x				7	6	-3	0	4					
4x		1	5	2				4	0				
6x		2	2	8					-3	8			
8x		3	0	4						2	1		

12. Since 21 < divisor, link 21 to next dividend digit to make 216.
    Since 216 ≥ divisor, find largest divisor multiple that is not greater than 216.
    This multiple is **152**, so sixth quotient digit is factor **4** corresponding to **152**.

							0	0	8	1	0	**4**	
1x				3	8	|	3	0	8	0	1	6	8
2x				7	6	-3	0	4					
4x		**1**	**5**	**2**				4	0				
6x		2	2	8					-3	8			
8x		3	0	4						2	1	6	

Good News Long Division Example 1

13. Subtract 152 from 216 to get 64.

```
                                      0   0   8   1   0   4
    1x            3   8 | 3   0   8   0   1   6   8
    2x            7   6  -3   0   4
    4x    1   5   2                  4   0
    6x    2   2   8                 -3   8
    8x    3   0   4                      2   1   6
                                        -1   5   2
                                             6   4
```

14. Since 64 ≥ divisor after subtraction of an even divisor multiple, subtract divisor from 64 to get 26. Add 1 to quotient digit 4. (Cross out 4; write 5 above it.)

```
                                                  5
                                      0   0   8   1   0   ̶4̶
    1x            3   8 | 3   0   8   0   1   6   8
    2x            7   6  -3   0   4
    4x    1   5   2                  4   0
    6x    2   2   8                 -3   8
    8x    3   0   4                      2   1   6
                                        -1   5   2
                                             6   4
                                            -3   8
                                             2   6
```

Warning: A difference that is not less than the divisor after subtracting the divisor indicates an error. Any such error must be found and corrected before proceeding.

Good News Long Division Example 1

15. Since 26 < divisor, link 26 to next dividend digit to make 268.
    Since 268 ≥ divisor, find largest divisor multiple that is ≤ 268.
    This multiple is **228**, so seventh quotient digit is factor **6** corresponding to **228**.

```
                                            5
                          0   0   8   1   0   4   6
    1x           3   8 | 3   0   8   0   1   6   8
    2x           7   6  -3   0   4
    4x       1   5   2           4   0
    6x       2   2   8          -3   8
    8x       3   0   4               2   1   6
                                    -1   5   2
                                         6   4
                                        -3   8
                                             2   6   8
```

16. Subtract 228 from 268 to get 40.

```
                                            5
                          0   0   8   1   0   4   6
    1x           3   8 | 3   0   8   0   1   6   8
    2x           7   6  -3   0   4
    4x       1   5   2           4   0
    6x       2   2   8          -3   8
    8x       3   0   4               2   1   6
                                    -1   5   2
                                         6   4
                                        -3   8
                                             2   6   8
                                            -2   2   8
                                                 4   0
```

55

Good News Long Division Example 1

17. Since 40 ≥ divisor after subtraction of an even divisor multiple, subtract divisor from 40 to get 2. Add 1 to quotient digit 6. (Cross out 6; write 7 above it.)

											5	7
					0	0	8	1	0	4	6̶
1x			3	8	3	0	8	0	1	6	8
2x			7	6	-3	0	4				
4x	1	5	2			4	0				
6x	2	2	8			-3	8				
8x	3	0	4				2	1	6		
							-1	5	2		
								6	4		
								-3	8		
								2	6	7	
								2	2	8	
									4	0	
									-3	8	
										2	

Good News Long Division Example 1

18. Since 2 < divisor and no dividend digits remain, the process ends with a remainder of 2. Write "R 2" next to the last quotient digit.

```
                                      5  7
                      0  0  8  1  0  4  6  R  2
  1x         3  8 | 3  0  8  0  1  6  8
  2x         7  6  -3  0  4
            ─────────────
  4x    1   5  2           4  0
  6x    2   2  8          -3  8
          ────
  8x    3   0  4                2  1  6
                               -1  5  2
                               ───────
                                   6  4
                                  -3  8
                                  ─────
                                      2  6  7
                                     -2  2  8
                                     ───────
                                         4  0
                                        -3  8
                                        ─────
                                            2
```

The figure below shows the figure above without shading.

```
                                      5  7
                      0  0  8  1  0  4  6  R  2
  1x         3  8 | 3  0  8  0  1  6  8
  2x         7  6  -3  0  4
                   ─────────
  4x    1   5  2           4  0
  6x    2   2  8          -3  8
                           ─────
  8x    3   0  4               2  1  6
                              -1  5  2
                              ───────
                                  6  4
                                 -3  8
                                 ─────
                                     2  6  8
                                    -2  2  8
                                    ───────
                                        4  0
                                       -3  8
                                       ─────
                                           2
```

Quotient = 81,057 with Remainder = 2

Good News Long Division Example 2

The following step-by-step example shows how to use Good News Long Division to divide 329,289,349 by 764. Each numbered instruction is followed by a figure that shows what needs to be done.

1. Write the division problem in standard form.

   ```
   7  6  4 | 3  2  9  2  8  9  3  4  9
   ```

2. Use doubling and addition to build the table of divisor multiples:
   764 + 764 = **1528**, 1528 + 1528 = **3056**, 3056 + 3056 = **6112**, and 1528 + 3056 = **4584**.

Table of Divisor Multiples	
Factor	Multiple
1x	7 6 4
2x	1 5 2 8
4x	3 0 5 6
6x	4 5 8 4
8x	6 1 1 2

   ```
              7  6  4 | 3  2  9  2  8  9  3  4  9
   ```

3. Start with the first dividend digit on the left and work right, one digit at a time. Since first dividend digit of 3 is less than divisor, first quotient digit is 0.

   ```
                              0
   1x         7  6  4 | 3  2  9  2  8  9  3  4  9
   2x      1  5  2  8
   ```

4. Since 3 < divisor, link the first two dividend digits to make 32.
   Since 32 < divisor, second dividend digit is 0.

   ```
                              0  0
   1x         7  6  4 | 3  2  9  2  8  9  3  4  9
   2x      1  5  2  8
   ```

Note: In this example, some of the steps shown in the first example have been combined, and most of the comments and warnings have not been repeated.

Good News Long Division Example 2

5. Since 32 < divisor, link the first three dividend digits to make 329.
   Since 329 < divisor, third dividend digit is 0.

   ```
                         0  0  0
   1x         7  6  4 | 3  2  9  2  8  9  3  4  9
   2x      1  5  2  8
   ```

6. Since 329 < divisor, link the first four dividend digits to make 3292.
   Since 3292 ≥ divisor, find largest divisor multiple that is ≤ 3292.
   This multiple is 3056, so fourth quotient digit is factor **4** corresponding to **3056**.

   ```
   factor      multiple        0  0  0  4
     1x          7  6  4 | 3  2  9  2  8  9  3  4  9
     2x       1  5  2  8
     4x       3  0  5  6
     6x       4  5  8  4
     8x       6  1  1  2
   ```

7. Subtract 3056 from 3292 to get **236**.

   ```
                               0  0  0  4
     1x          7  6  4 | 3  2  9  2  8  9  3  4  9
     2x       1  5  2  8  -3  0  5  6
     4x       3  0  5  6         2  3  6
     6x       4  5  8  4
     8x       6  1  1  2
   ```

Good News Long Division Example 2

8. Since 236 < divisor, link 236 to next dividend digit to make 2368.
   Since 2368 ≥ divisor, find largest divisor multiple that is ≤ 2368.
   This multiple is 1528, so fifth quotient digit is factor **2** corresponding to **1528**.

						0	0	0	4	2			
1x			7	6	4	3	2	9	2	8	9	3	4	9
2x	1	5	2	8		-3	0	5	6				
4x	3	0	5	6			2	3	6	8			
6x	4	5	8	4									
8x	6	1	1	2									

9. Subtract 1528 from 2368 to get 840.

						0	0	0	4	2			
1x			7	6	4	3	2	9	2	8	9	3	4	9
2x	1	5	2	8		-3	0	5	6				
4x	3	0	5	6			2	3	6	8			
6x	4	5	8	4			-1	5	2	8			
8x	6	1	1	2				8	4	0			

Good News Long Division Example 2

10. Since 840 ≥ divisor after subtracting an even divisor multiple, subtract divisor from 840 to get 76. Add 1 to fifth quotient digit 2. (Cross out 2; write 3 above it.)

										3			
					0	0	0	4	~~2~~			
1x			7	6	4	3	2	9	2	8	9	3	4	9
2x	1	5	2	8	-3	0	5	6					
4x	3	0	5	6			2	3	6	8			
6x	4	5	8	4			-1	5	2	8			
8x	6	1	1	2				8	4	0			
								-7	6	4			
									7	6			

11. Since 76 < divisor, link 76 to next dividend digit to get 769.
    Since 769 ≥ divisor, find largest divisor multiple that is not greater than 769.
    This multiple is 764, so sixth quotient digit is factor **1** corresponding to **764**.

										3				
					0	0	0	4	~~2~~	1			
1x			7	6	4	3	2	9	2	8	9	3	4	9
2x	1	5	2	8	-3	0	5	6						
4x	3	0	5	6			2	3	6	8				
6x	4	5	8	4			-1	5	2	8				
8x	6	1	1	2				8	4	0				
								-7	6	4				
									7	6	9			

Good News Long Division Example 2

12. Subtract 764 from 769 to get 5.

```
                                    3
                        0  0  0  4  2  1
1x          7  6  4  | 3  2  9  2  8  9  3  4  9
2x       1  5  2  8   -3  0  5  6
4x       3  0  5  6      2  3  6  8
6x       4  5  8  4     -1  5  2  8
8x       6  1  1  2         8  4  0
                           -7  6  4
                               7  6  9
                              -7  6  4
                                     5
```

13. Since 5 < divisor, link 5 to next dividend digit to get 53.
    Since 53 < divisor, seventh quotient digit is 0.

```
                                       3
                        0  0  0  4  2  1  0
1x          7  6  4  | 3  2  9  2  8  9  3  4  9
2x       1  5  2  8   -3  0  5  6
4x       3  0  5  6      2  3  6  8
6x       4  5  8  4     -1  5  2  8
8x       6  1  1  2         8  4  0
                           -7  6  4
                               7  6  9
                              -7  6  4
                                  5  3
```

Good News Long Division Example 2

14. Since 53 < divisor, link 53 to next dividend digit to get 534.
    Since 534 < divisor, eighth quotient digit is 0.

```
                              3
                      0 0 0 4 2̶ 1 0 0
  1x         7 6 4 | 3 2 9 2 8 9 3 4 9
  2x     1 5 2 8   -3 0 5 6
  4x     3 0 5 6       2 3 6 8
  6x     4 5 8 4      -1 5 2 8
  8x     6 1 1 2           8 4 0
                          -7 6 4
                               7 6 9
                              -7 6 4
                                 5 3 4
```

15. Since 534 < divisor, link 534 to next dividend digit to get 5349.
    Since 5349 ≥ divisor, find largest divisor multiple that is ≤ 5349.
    This multiple is 4584, so ninth quotient digit is **6** corresponding to **4584**.

```
                              3
                      0 0 0 4 2̶ 1 0 0 6
  1x         7 6 4 | 3 2 9 2 8 9 3 4 9
  2x     1 5 2 8   -3 0 5 6
  4x     3 0 5 6       2 3 6 8
  6x     4 5 8 4      -1 5 2 8
  8x     6 1 1 2           8 4 0
                          -7 6 4
                               7 6 9
                              -7 6 4
                                 5 3 4 9
```

Good News Long Division Example 2

16. Subtract 4584 from 5349 to get 765.

```
                                3
                      0  0  0  4  2̶  1  0  0  6
1x        7  6  4 |  3  2  9  2  8  9  3  4  9
2x    1   5  2  8   -3  0  5  6
4x    3   0  5  6       2  3  6  8
6x    4   5  8  4      -1  5  2  8
8x    6   1  1  2          8  4  0
                          -7  6  4
                              7  6  9
                             -7  6  4
                                    5  3  4  9
                                   -4  5  8  4
                                       7  6  5
```

17. Since 765 ≥ divisor after subtracting an even divisor multiple, subtract divisor from 765 to get 1. Add 1 to ninth quotient digit 6. (Cross out 6; write 7 above it.)

```
                                3              7
                      0  0  0  4  2̶  1  0  0  6̶
1x        7  6  4 |  3  2  9  2  8  9  3  4  9
2x    1   5  2  8   -3  0  5  6
4x    3   0  5  6       2  3  6  8
6x    4   5  8  4      -1  5  2  8
8x    6   1  1  2          8  4  0
                          -7  6  4
                              7  6  9
                             -7  6  4
                                    5  3  4  9
                                   -4  5  8  4
                                       7  6  5
                                      -7  6  4
                                             1
```

Good News Long Division Example 2

18. Since 1 < divisor and no dividend digits remain, the process ends with a remainder of 1. Write "R 1" next to the last quotient digit.

```
                                          3              7
                            0   0   0   4  2̶   1   0   0  6̶   R  1
   1x        7  6  4 │ 3   2   9   2   8   9   3   4   9
   2x   1   5  2  8   -3   0   5   6
   4x   3   0  5  6        2   3   6   8
   6x   4   5  8  4       -1   5   2   8
   8x   6   1  1  2            8   4   0
                              -7   6   4
                                   7   6   9
                                  -7   6   4
                                           5   3   4   9
                                          -4   5   8   4
                                               7   6   5
                                              -7   6   4
                                                       1
```

Quotient = 431,007 with Remainder = 1

Checking Good News Long Division

Good News Long Division is verified the same way that traditional long division is verified:

$$\text{Dividend} = (\text{Divisor} \times \text{Quotient}) + \text{Remainder}.$$

A table of divisors multiples and the expanded form of the quotient are needed because the divisor is the multiplicand and the quotient is the multiplier in the above formula. (See sections 5 and 6.)

Check Good News Long Division as follows:
1. Use the table of divisor multiples from the division problem.
2. Create the expanded form of the quotient somewhere in the work area.
3. Use Good News Multiplication to multiply: Divisor x Quotient.
4. Add the division Remainder to the Step 3 product.
5. The division result is correct if the Step 4 sum equals the dividend.

   Warning: Be sure that the table of divisor multiples has been checked before it is used again to check the division problem.

Checking Good News Long Division

The example below shows how to check Good News Long Division with Good News Multiplication.

Good News Long Division with Checking

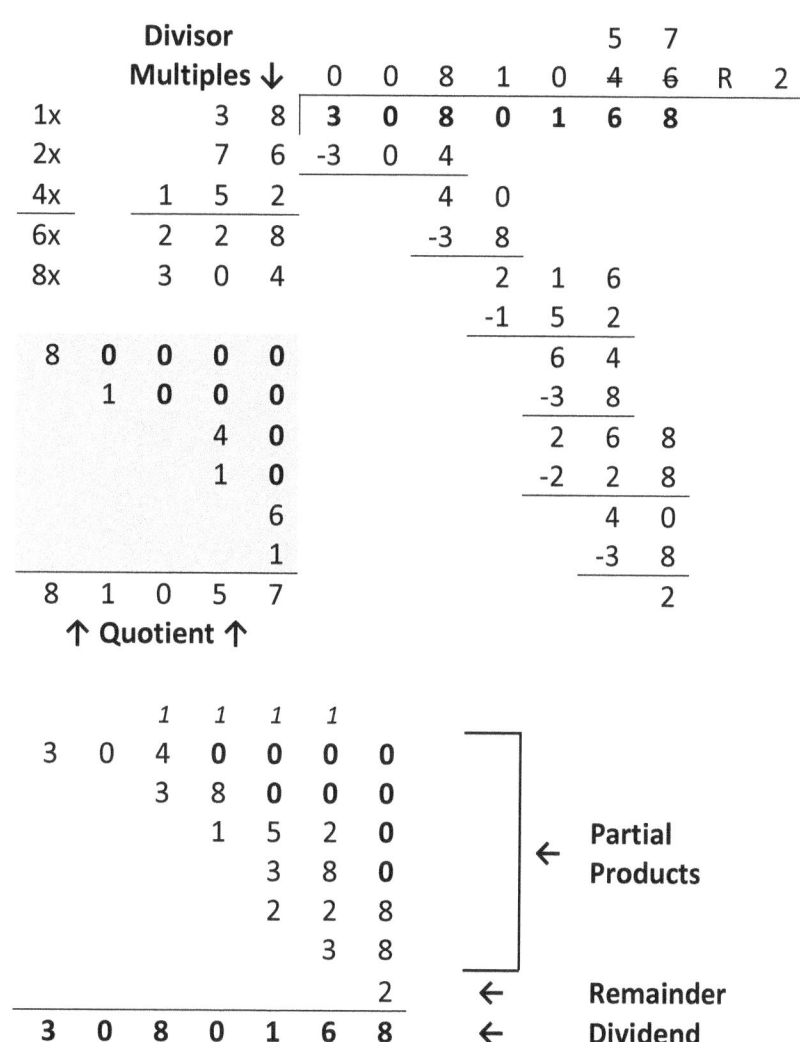

The shaded area above is the expanded quotient.

Note: Each partial product equals the divisor times the corresponding row of the expanded quotient.

Single-digit Divisor Example

This example shows all the concepts involved in Good News Long Division. The example is relatively easy to follow because the numbers involved in the subtractions are small.

							9		7		**5**		3					
				0	8̶	8	6̶	6	0	0	**4**	4	2̶	2	1	R	1
1x			9	8	8	8	8	4	0	4	**8**	8	8	9	0		
2x		1	8	-7	2												
4x		3	6	1	6												
6x		5	4	-9													
8x		7	2	7	8												
				-7	2												
					6	8											
					-5	4											
					1	4											
						-9											
						5	4										
						-5	4										
						0	0	4	**8**								
								-3	**6**								
								1	**2**								
									-9								
									3	8							
									-3	6							
										2	8						
										-1	8						
										1	0						
											-9						
											1	9					
											-1	8					
												1	0				
												-9					
												1					

Warning: Cross out dividend digits as they are used.

When dividend digits repeat, it is easy to skip one or use it twice.

Single-digit Divisor Example

In the example on the previous page, notice that the low-order digit of each subtracted divisor multiple vertically aligns with two other numbers: the last dividend digit used to make the number from which it is subtracted and the quotient digit associated with it. See the shaded column for quotient digit **5** in the figure on the preceding page.

Dividend digits have not been crossed out in any examples of completed calculations shown in this book. The value of crossing out dividend digits is only apparent in the midst of a calculation when some dividend digits have been used and are crossed out while others have not been used and are not crossed out.

Short division is probably more efficient division method for single-digit divisors, but it requires accurate recall of the basic multiplication tables and some mental math. However, Good News Long Division involves no multiplication and very little mental math.

11 Division Examples

Single-digit Divisors

				4	
1x			2	8	
2x			4	-8	
4x			8	0	
6x	1	2			
8x	1	6			

				3	5		
				2̶	4	R	1
1x			2	7	1		
2x			4	-4			
4x			8	3			
6x	1	2		-1			
8x	1	6		1	1		
					-8		
					3		
					-2		
					1		

				3	7		
			0	2̶	6̶	R	2
1x			3	1	3		
2x			6	-6			
4x	1	2		5			
6x	1	8		-3			
8x	2	4		2	3		
				-1	8		
					5		
					-3		
					2		

				9		5	
			0	8̶	0	4̶	
1x			4	3	6	2	0
2x			8	-3	2		
4x	1	6		4			
6x	2	4		-4			
8x	3	2		0	2	0	
					-1	6	
						4	
						-4	
						0	

Single-digit Divisors

```
                          5   5       3
                    0   4 4   0   2 R 3
1x          5 | 2   7   5   1   8
2x    1   0  -2   0
4x    2   0       7
6x    3   0      -5
8x    4   0       2   5
                 -2   0
                      5
                     -5
                      0   1   8
                         -1   0
                              8
                             -5
                              3


                          5       7
                    0   8 4   0   6 R 2
1x          6 | 5   1   0   4   4
2x    1   2  -4   8
4x    2   4       3   0
6x    3   6      -2   4
8x    4   8       6
                 -6
                  0   4   4
                     -3   6
                          8
                         -6
                          2
```

Single-digit Divisors

```
                              3
                    1  0  0  8  2̶  R  1
1x         7 | 7  0  5  8  2
2x      1  4  -7
4x      2  8     0  5  8
6x      4  2        -5  6
8x      5  6            2  2
                       -1  4
                           8
                          -7
                           1


                           5        9
                    0  2  4  0  8  8̶  R  3
1x         8 | 2  0  0  7  1  5
2x      1  6  -1  6
4x      3  2     4  0
6x      4  8    -3  2
8x      6  4        8
                   -8
                    0  7  1
                      -6  4
                          7  5
                         -6  4
                             1  1
                                -8
                                 3
```

72

Single-digit Divisors

								3	7		
				0	2	1	0	2̶	6̶	R	1
1x			9 ⌐	1	8	9	3	4	8	4	
2x	1	8	-1	8							
4x	3	6				9					
6x	5	4				-9					
8x	7	2				0	3	4			
							-1	8			
							1	6			
							-9				
							7	8			
							-7	2			
								6	4		
								-5	4		
								1	0		
									-9		
									1		

										9	
				0	6	0	0	2	1	4	8̶
1x			9 ⌐| 5	4	0	1	9	3	4	0	1
2x	1	8	-5	4							
4x	3	6		0	0	1	9				
6x	5	4				-1	8				
8x	7	2					1	3			
								-9			
								4	4		
								-3	6		
									8	0	
									-7	2	
										8	1
										-7	2
											9
											-9
											0

Two-digit Divisors

```
                        3   5
                0   2   4   8   R   1
1x          1  7│ 6   0   8   7
2x          3  4 -3   4
4x          6  8  2   6
6x      1   0  2 -1   7
8x      1   3  6      9   8
                     -6   8
                      3   0
                     -1   7
                      1   3   7
                     -1   3   6
                              1
```

```
                        7       5
                0   0   6   4   0   4   1   R   0
1x           8  5│ 6   2   9   4   3   3   5
2x       1   7  0 -5   1   0
4x       3   4  0  1   1   9
6x       5   1  0     -8   5
8x       6   8  0      3   4   4
                      -3   4   0
                           4   3   3
                          -3   4   0
                               9   3
                              -8   5
                                   8   5
                                  -8   5
                                       0
```

Note: Grid lines are not shown to avoid distraction and more clearly focus on the process.

Two-digit Divisors

```
                                    5
                          0  0  6   1  0  4  R 2
    1x         4  9 | 2   9  9   1  4  7
    2x         9  8  -2   9  4
    4x      1  9  6           5  1
    6x      2  9  4          -4  9
    8x      3  9  2             2  4  7
                               -1  9  6
                                   5  1
                                  -4  9
                                      2
```

```
                              9       3
                           0  0  8  4  0  2  1  R 0
    1x         6  8 | 6   3  9  4  1  0  8
    2x      1  3  6  -5   4  4
    4x      2  7  2       9  5
    6x      4  0  8      -6  8
    8x      5  4  4         2  7  4
                           -2  7  2
                                  2  1  0
                                 -1  3  6
                                     7  4
                                    -6  8
                                        6  8
                                       -6  8
                                           0
```

Three-digit Divisors

```
                                            5  7
                            0  0  1  2  0   4  6  R 3
   1x            1  6  8 | 2  0  2  5  5  7  9
   2x            3  3  6  -1  6  8
   4x            6  7  2     3  4  5
   6x         1  0  0  8    -3  3  6
   8x         1  3  4  4           9  5  7
                                  -6  7  2
                                   2  8  5
                                  -1  6  8
                                   1  1  7  9
                                  -1  0  0  8
                                         1  7  1
                                        -1  6  8
                                               3
```

```
                                         3        5
                            0  0  0  2  8  0  0   4  R 11
   1x            5  4  6 | 2  0  7  5  0  7  4  1
   2x         1  0  9  2  -1  0  9  2
   4x         2  1  8  4     9  8  3
   6x         3  2  7  6    -5  4  6
   8x         4  3  6  8     4  3  7  0
                            -4  3  6  8
                                      2  7  4  1
                                     -2  1  8  4
                                         5  5  7
                                        -5  4  6
                                               1  1
```

76

Three-digit Divisors

```
                              7           9
                    0  0  0  8  6  0  4  0  8  R  0
1x           6 4 3 |5  5  9  6  7  2  9  8  7
2x       1 2 8 6   -5  1  4  4
4x       2 5 7 2    4  5  2  7
6x       3 8 5 8   -3  8  5  8
8x       5 1 4 4       6  6  9
                      -6  4  3
                       2  6  2  9
                      -2  5  7  2
                          5  7  8  7
                         -5  1  4  4
                             6  4  3
                            -6  4  3
                                 0
```

```
                           9  7        3  5
                    0  0  0  8  6  0  1  1  2  4  R  7
1x           8 7 2 |8  4  5  9  3  8  9  7  2  7
2x       1 7 4 4   -6  9  7  6
4x       3 4 8 8    1  4  8  3
6x       5 2 3 2      -8  7  2
8x       6 9 7 6       6  1  1  3
                      -5  2  3  2
                          8  8  1
                         -8  7  2
                             9  8  9
                            -8  7  2
                             1  1  7  7
                               -8  7  2
                                3  0  5  2
                               -1  7  4  4
                                1  3  0  8
                                  -8  7  2
                                   4  3  6  7
                                  -3  4  8  8
                                      8  7  9
                                     -8  7  2
                                         7
```

77

Four-digit Divisors

```
                                        9
                             0  0  0  0  6  8  0  0  1  0  R 3
  1x           1  9  0  8 | 1  3  1  6  5  3  9  0  8  3
  2x           3  8  1  6  -1  1  4  4  8
  4x           7  6  3  2     1  7  1  7  3
  6x        1  1  4  4  8    -1  5  2  6  4
  8x        1  5  2  6  4        1  9  0  9
                                -1  9  0  8
                                    1  9  0  8
                                   -1  9  0  8
                                           0  3
```

```
                                        3              5
                             0  0  0  0  2  4  0  0  0  4  2  R 1
  1x           9  8  0  7 | 3  3  3  4  4  3  0  9  9  6  5
  2x        1  9  6  1  4  -1  9  6  1  4
  4x        3  9  2  2  8     1  3  7  3  0
  6x        5  8  8  4  2       -9  8  0  7
  8x        7  8  4  5  6        3  9  2  3  3
                                -3  9  2  2  8
                                          5  0  9  9  6
                                         -3  9  2  2  8
                                             1  1  7  6  8
                                               -9  8  0  7
                                                   1  9  6  1  5
                                                  -1  9  6  1  4
                                                              1
```

Five-digit Divisors

```
                                            3           3
                          0  0  0  0  2  0  1  4  2  8  R 2
1x        1  0  6  7  8 | 3  2  1  8  7  5  4  9  6  6
2x        2  1  3  5  6  -2  1  3  5  6
4x        4  2  7  1  2     1  0  8  3  1
6x        6  4  0  6  8    -1  0  6  7  8
8x        8  5  4  2  4        1  5  3  5  4
                              -1  0  6  7  8
                                  4  6  7  6  9
                                 -4  2  7  1  2
                                     4  0  5  7  6
                                    -2  1  3  5  6
                                        1  9  2  2  0
                                       -1  0  6  7  8
                                           8  5  4  2  6
                                          -8  5  4  2  4
                                                       2
```

```
                                               5
                          0  0  0  0  0  6  0  8  4  1  R 1
1x           8  4  5  6  2 | 5  1  4  5  6  8  2  2  6  3
2x        1  6  9  1  2  4 -5  0  7  3  7  2
4x        3  3  8  2  4  8     7  1  9  6  2  2
6x        5  0  7  3  7  2    -6  7  6  4  9  6
8x        6  7  6  4  9  6        4  3  1  2  6  6
                                 -3  3  8  2  4  8
                                     9  3  0  1  8
                                    -8  4  5  6  2
                                        8  4  5  6  3
                                       -8  4  5  6  2
                                                    1
```

Final Division Example

Below is an example of an eleven-digit number divided by a five-digit number with complete checking. Try this problem using traditional long division and multiplication.

```
                                            3 5       9
                          0 0 0 0 0 6 2 4 2 0 8 R 5
 1x      3 9 2 8 7 | 2 4 9 5 5 4 5 5 9 8 8
 2x      7 8 5 7 4  -2 3 5 7 2 2
 4x    1 5 7 1 4 8    1 3 8 3 2 5
 6x    2 3 5 7 2 2     -7 8 5 7 4
 8x    3 1 4 2 9 6      5 9 7 5 1
14x    5 5 0 0 1 8     -3 9 2 8 7
-4x   -1 5 7 1 4 8      2 0 4 6 4 5
10x    3 9 2 8 7 0     -1 5 7 1 4 8
                          4 7 4 9 7
                         -3 9 2 8 7
                            8 2 1 0 9
                           -7 8 5 7 4
                            3 5 3 5 8 8
                           -3 1 4 2 9 6
                              3 9 2 9 2
                             -3 9 2 8 7
                                    5
```

Table of Multiples Check

The shaded zeros below are place-holder zeros.

Expanded Quotient

```
6 0 0 0 0 0        1 3 3 3 3 3   1 1
  2 0 0 0 0      2 3 5 7 2 2 0 0 0 0 0
    1 0 0 0 0      7 8 5 7 4 0 0 0 0
      4 0 0 0      3 9 2 8 7 0 0 0
        1 0 0     1 5 7 1 4 8 0 0
          2 0       3 9 2 8 7 0 0
            8         7 8 5 7 4 0
            1         3 1 4 2 9 6
6 3 5 2 0 9           3 9 2 8 7
                                5 ← R
                  2 4 9 5 5 4 5 5 9 8 8
```
Dividend Check

Good News Long Division requires **no memorization** of multiplication tables, **no guessing** or estimating of quotient digits, and **no multiplication**.
Good News Multiplication involves no multiplication.

 # Blank Page #

12 Fast Track

This section summarizes Good News Multiplication and Good News Long Division with one example of each. Reading the other sections of this book may be unnecessary if these two pages provide the reader with enough information to use the Good News algorithms correctly.

Good News Multiplication Summary Example

1. Put a table of multiplicand multiples under the multiplicand. The multiples are produced by addition: 2367 + 2367 = 4734, 4734 + 4734 = 9468, 9468 + 9468 = 18936, and 4734 + 9468 = 14202.
2. Expand the multiplier vertically under itself with digits 3, 5, 7, and 9 replaced by the next smaller even digit and a one beneath this even digit. See the numbers in the box below. The shaded numbers are place-holder zeros.
3. For each row of the expanded multiplier, do the following:
    a. Match the row's first digit to a factor in the table of multiplicand multiples and get the multiple corresponding to this factor.
    b. Make a partial product by putting the same number of zeros in the expanded multiplier row on the right side of the multiple from Step 3a.
4. Total the partial products to get the multiplication product.

Table of Multiplicand Multiples							Expanded Multiplier					Partial Products							
Factor	Multiple																		
1x		2	3	6	7	x	7	0	5	4									
2x		4	7	3	4		6	0	0	0		1	4	2	0	2	**0**	**0**	**0**
4x		9	4	6	8		1	0	0	0			2	3	6	7	**0**	**0**	**0**
6x	1	4	2	0	2				4	0				9	4	6	8	**0**	
8x	1	8	9	3	6				1	0				2	3	6	7	**0**	
										4					9	4	6	8	
							7	0	5	4		1	6	6	9	6	8	1	8

2,367 x 7,054 = 16,696,818

Fast Track

Good News Long Division Summary

1. Put a table of divisor multiples under the divisor. The multiples are produced by addition: 367 + 367 = 734, 734 + 734 = 1468, 1468 + 1468 = 2936, and 734 + 1468 = 2202. The initial remaining dividend (RD) is the given dividend.
2. Repeat Steps 3 – 7 until RD is less than the divisor.
3. Make a number that is not less than the divisor from the smallest series of high-order digits in RD. Call the last dividend digit in this series LD.
4. Find the largest multiple in the Table of Divisor Multiples that does not exceed the step-3 number. Subtract it from the step-3 number.
5. The quotient digit is the factor from the Table of Divisor Multiples that corresponds to the step-3 multiple. Put it above dividend in vertical alignment with LD and the low-order digit of the subtracted step-3 multiple.
6. If the step-4 difference is not less than the divisor, subtract the divisor from the step-4 difference, and add one to the step-5 quotient digit.
7. Make a new RD by linking all dividend digits to the right of LD to the right side of the last subtraction difference, which may come from either step 4 or step 6.
8. A zero quotient digit appears above any dividend digit that does not have a low-order digit of a subtracted divisor multiple in vertical alignment with it.

Table of Divisor Multiples												
Factor	Multiple				0	0	0	**5** **4**	0	4	1	**9** 8 R 2
1x		3	6	7	1	8	5	**0**	3	7	7	5
2x		7	3	4	-1	4	6	8				
4x	1	4	6	8		3	8	**2**				
6x	2	2	0	2		-3	6	**7**				
8x	2	9	3	6			1	**5**	3	7		
							-1	4	6	8		
								6	9	7		
								-3	6	7		
								3	3	0	5	
								-2	9	3	6	
Quotient = 50,419									3	6	9	
Remainder = 2									-3	6	7	
											2	

13 Methods Compared

Multiplication Methods Compared

Traditional Multiplication

```
            6  3  1
            3  2  1
            2  1              ← Multiplication Carries
         3  7  4  2
       x    9  5  4
      1  1  1                 ← Addition Carries
         1  4  9  6  8
      1  8  7  1  0  0
   3  3  6  7  8  0  0
   3  5  6  9  8  6  8
```

Good News Multiplication

```
1x            3  7  4  2   x  9  5  4
2x            7  4  8  4
4x         1  4  9  6  8
6x         2  2  4  5  2
8x         2  9  9  3  6
```

```
                  1  2  2  2  1     ← Addition Carries
      8        2  9  9  3  6  0  0
      1           3  7  4  2  0  0
         4        1  4  9  6  8  0
         1           3  7  4  2  0
            4           1  4  9  6  8
      9  5  4     3  5  6  9  8  6  8
```

Traditional multiplication relies on accurate recall of basic multiplication tables and considerable mental math, which makes it very prone to errors.

Good News Multiplication involves absolutely **no multiplication** and relatively little mental math. It is also **easy to check**.

Division Methods with Single-digit Divisors Compared

Comparison of Three Methods of Division
By a Single-digit Divisor

Traditional Long Division

```
        0  5  7  9  3  R  1
     7│ 4  0  5  5  3
       -3  5
           5  5
          -4  9
              6  5
             -6  3
                 2  3
                -2  1
                    2
```

Good News Long Division

```
               5  7  9  3
            0  4  6  8  2  R  1
     1x  7│ 4  0  5  5  3
     2x  14  -2  8
     4x  28      1  2
     6x  42     -7
     8x  56         5  5
                   -4  2
                       1  3
                      -7
                       6  5
                      -5  6
                          9
                         -7
                          2  3
                         -1  4
                             8
                            -7
                             1
```

Short Division

```
           0  5   7   9   3  R  3
        7│ 4  ⁴0  ⁵5  ⁶5  ²3
```

Short Division is probably the most efficient division method for single-digit divisors. However, both traditional long division and short division depend on accurate recall of basic multiplication tables and considerable mental-math.

Good News Long Division requires no multiplication and less mental math. However, it is somewhat cumbersome for single-digit divisors.

Traditional Long Division and Good News Long Division Compared

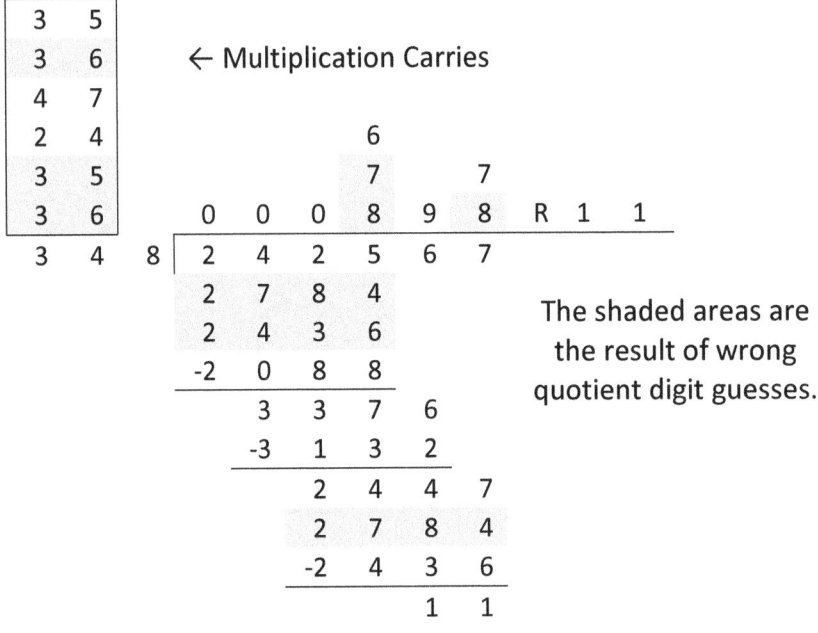

Good News Long Division involves **no guessing** and **no multiplication**. It is **easy to check** and **very powerful**. Traditional long division requires guessing quotient digits and testing the guesses with multiplication, so it is very error prone and hard to check.

Good News Long Division **difficulty increases only slightly as divisors get bigger** while traditional long division difficulty increases dramatically as divisors get bigger.

14 Blank Grid Forms

The next three unnumbered pages contain blank grid forms in three different grid sizes. These forms may be copied and used for practice problems.

Using grid paper when learning the Good News algorithms minimizes the distraction of trying to keep columns of digits properly aligned.